THE ABUNDANT AUTHOR *Playbook*

A guide to creating an abundant business around your book

NICOLA HUMBER

Copyright © 2025 by Nicola Humber

All rights reserved. No part of this publication may be reproduced, distributed or transmitted in any form or by any means without permission of the publisher, except in the case of brief quotations referencing the body of work and in accordance with copyright law.

The information given in this book should not be treated as a substitute for professional medical advice; always consult a medical practitioner. Any use of information in this book is at the reader's discretion and risk. Neither the author nor the publisher can be held responsible for any loss, claim or damage arising out of the use, or misuse, of the suggestions made, the failure to take medical advice or for any material on third party websites.

ISBN:

(Paperback) 978-1-916529-44-1

 (ebook) 978-1-916529-45-8

Cover design by Lynda Mangoro.

The Unbound Press
www.theunboundpress.com

Hey unbound one!

Welcome to this magical book brought to you by The Unbound Press.

At The Unbound Press we believe that when women write freely from the fullest expression of who they are, it can't help but activate a feeling of deep connection and transformation in others. When we come together, we become more and we're changing the world, one book at a time!

This book has been carefully crafted by both the author and publisher with the intention of inspiring you to move ever more deeply into who you truly are.

We hope that this book helps you to connect with your Unbound Self and that you feel called to pass it on to others who want to live a more fully expressed life.

With much love,

Nicola Humber

Founder of The Unbound Press

www.theunboundpress.com

For Mr H, my partner on this unbound journey.

Your book is a seed.

Whether you're thinking about writing one, are in the process or it's already out in the world (*and in that case, go you magical one!*), your book has latent potential; possibly more than you can imagine.

Of course, the book in itself is powerful.

The words within it get to create connection, activation, insight + deepened awareness for each reader (and you as the author).

But the premise of this book is that's just the beginning.

Why I Felt Called to Write This Book

As an author myself, writing mentor and founder of a publishing community, I've become more and more frustrated that SO many magical authors don't benefit fully from the huge amount of time and energy they pour into writing their brilliant books. After the initial buzz of the launch, there can be a feeling of anti-climax – is that it? – as they drift back into post-book life.

Maybe an author will share snippets about their book in the weeks and months afterwards, but often it gets neglected. Many writers end up disappointed with the number of sales their book has made and can even feel ashamed that this project they've put their heart and soul into hasn't manifested the results they expected or desired.

If that's you, or you have a fear of this happening, I want you to know you're not alone. And what you've experienced (or are fearful of) is very normal. People think that writing and publishing a book is some kind of magic pill. And it IS in many ways, but probably not in the way you expect.

This playbook has been created out of my desire for more magical writers to be able to activate wild abundance through their books. In these pages I'm going to give you a set of invitations, a (relatively simple) process to move through in order to:

- Step more fully into the Abundant Author you're here to be (the Abundant Author you already ARE)
- Bring more (and more) soul-aligned people into your world
- Create an offer that amplifies the message of your book
- Launch the offer in a way that deepens connection with your people
- Uncover ways to expand your field of impact through joy-full co-creation and collaboration

How does that sound?

So, as we land here together, let me ask you a couple of questions to get some juices flowing:

When you imagine your book as a seed that you get to plant, what does it want to become?

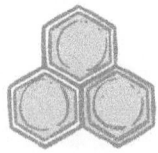

What does it want to be the foundation for?

_____
_____
_____
_____
_____
_____
_____

Take some time to ponder, magical one. Let what wants to come, come.

We'll be exploring this much, MUCH more throughout these pages. But as we begin, I want you to know your book has an energy, an essence, a blueprint of its own. It has a unique mission here on earth that it wants to fulfil. And it needs you to do that.

What this Book Is NOT

This is not a book about how to become a bestseller or sell more copies of your book. That may be a by-product of the process I'll be guiding you through, but my focus is helping you create a way for abundance to flow to you in substantial amounts. (We'll be talking more about what abundance is and the different forms it takes, but my main intention is that you'll have access to (much) more financial abundance.)

So many authors get hung up on book sales. (Believe me, I've been there.) We can make those numbers mean all kinds of things about our worth as a writer + creator. But this is an incredibly limited perspective. Like I said, the book is just the beginning and your book sales are the tip of the iceberg.

So, what does it mean to be an Abundant Author?

And how do you get to claim that title for yourself?

That's what we'll be exploring in the pages of this book.

In truth, there are a quadrillion different ways you could open up channels of abundance based on your book and the work you're here to do in the world. Maybe that's why you've struggled in the past? Because trying to decide which route to take can feel overwhelming.

I know that feeling. Believe me, I've tried pretty much EVERYTHING since I started my own business back in 2010. When I (finally) followed the call to write my book(s), I thought I'd found the answer. Yes! This was going to change everything and the way would become clear.

Spoiler alert: Dear reader, that's not (quite) what happened next. My books did absolutely lead me more deeply on to my soul path. I ended up running a publishing company for goddess' sake! That was never part of the plan. And it's through my books that I managed to reach that elusive goal of creating a six-figure business.

But the books alone weren't enough. I had to allow them to become the foundation for other offerings and creations.

I had to see them as a way to connect with more of my soul-aligned people and create community.

I had to plant them like seeds and let them grow into what they truly wanted to be.

That's where the abundance lay.

What I'm not going to do in this book is give you a guided tour of everything I've tried over the past 14+ years of running my own business. I trust that if you're here, you'll benefit from hearing more about the golden thread that's flowed through everything and opened up abundance to me in new, expansive ways.

I'm specifically going to be taking you through a process that's based not only on harnessing the power of your book and what it wants to become, but also community.

Community has been an important theme in each of my books. It's been key to the success of my business. And this is the way I believe we can all benefit from following – bringing people together with a shared vision, creating connection and knowing that when we come together, we become more.

You can absolutely use the Abundant Author process to create and sell one-to-one offerings in your business, but everything I'm sharing with you in these pages will be through the lens of community.

Whether it's how to be more visible, what offer to create, how to launch that offer or how to reach new audiences, I'll be inviting you to focus on connection through community.

As we move into the Aquarian Age, it's time for us to realise we don't have to do this alone. Everything we do and create holds the potential of creating deeper connection – with ourselves, with our people and with the collective.

But before we dive into ALL that good stuff, let me tell you a little about my own experience and where it all began…

In the Beginning

Did I ever decide to start my own business? Nope. That was never the motivation.

I was moving away from, rather than moving towards; looking for something other than the monotony of the 9-5 I was in.

When I (pretty randomly, tbh) landed on the idea of retraining as a hypnotherapist, the business side of it didn't even enter my head. I was focused on the therapy side – going on my own journey of training and self-development. In my mind I saw myself setting up a hypnotherapy practice and that would be it. Clients would come. I'd see them for hour-long sessions. And that scenario would continue ad infinitum.

Simple.

But of course it wasn't.

We were given a couple of hours of 'business training' on the last weekend of my hypnotherapy course. And my degree is in Business Studies. So surely I'd be fine when it came to the business side?

But two things scuppered me with the 'this will be simple' approach:

1) My reliance on the belief that 'if you build it, they will come'.

2) My seemingly never-ending capacity for desiring growth, expansion, creative expression and new experiences.

My Unbound Self was never going to let it be simple!

I remember waking up the Monday morning after I'd passed my hypnotherapy assessment. I was in my then boyfriend's (now husband's) bed. He'd gone to work and the sun was cascading through the window.

I felt similarly to the way I'd done the night I got my degree results back in 1994. Dancing in the Student Union as Blur performed 'Parklife' on the stage, drinking lager from a plastic pint glass and celebrating with friends.

This was it! I'd done it. And my whole life stretched out in front of me. Luxuriously. Spaciously.

It was all set to be a glorious coast downhill from now on, surely?

The naivety.

Both of those moments were just the beginning. Because, of course, EVERY moment is a beginning.

The journey is continually evolving. We never fully arrive (even when we think we have).

And running your own business is one of the wildest journeys of all.

You might go into it with concerns around making enough money and getting your admin on track. But that's just the tip of a very freaking large iceberg.

You are on a train to transformation central my friend. And all of your shiz will be bubbling up along the way.

It's very similar to the book-writing process. On the surface it looks like it should be relatively simple. But with both – your book and your business – you're called to become more YOU.

Each step you take will help you remember more about who you are and what you're (really) here to do. And we're going to be diving into ALL that good stuff on this Abundant Author journey.

Start Where You Are

My invitation with the Abundant Author process is to give yourself permission to start where you feel called.

Maybe you write your book, know exactly what's contained therein and wait until it's out in the world to start embodying and expressing the Abundant Author you're here to be?

Maybe you have the faintest glimmering of a knowing that you're meant to write a book, that you ARE an author, somewhere on your timeline, and you feel called to start embodying the most abundant expression of your author self now?

Maybe you're at a point somewhere between these two?

It doesn't matter. You're here.

There's so much that doesn't matter that we make matter. And so much that DOES matter we ignore.

This is a side note – I'm prone to those – but I remember a few years ago receiving the message, 'Turn everything on its head'.

It kinda made sense at the time, but it makes more and more sense every day as we journey through whatever we're experiencing as a collective now.

Anyway, I digress. But I guess the invitation I'm extending to you in these pages is to turn much of what you've learned previously on its head. Certainly any old stories or limited ideas about who you are and what you're here to do, about whether you are an author or not (you are), about whether your work has value (it does), about whether there are people who want to receive what you have to offer (there 100% are!).

And I'm not being flippant. I know in my bones that this is true for you, magical one.

You might say, 'But you don't know me at all, Nicola'.

And to that, I say, 'I trust you've found your way here, to this book, to this page, precisely because it IS true for you'.

You are an author (and you get to be an abundant one).

Your work has immense value.

And there are people who are longing to receive what you have to offer.

That is the belief, the knowing I have for each of my readers. And you are one of them. So it's true for you.

Borrow my knowing for now, if you need to.

So what is an Abundant Author? You tell me, my friend.

Because it will mean something different to everyone who lands here. What I do know is that the abundance I talk of isn't just financial – it's creative, spiritual, physical, relational, ALL the flavours.

But I will be focusing on financial abundance a lot of the time in these pages. It's potent to have a focus. And I have a personal interest in you becoming (more) financially abundant.

I want you to buy more of my books.

Ha! Only jesting.

I want more money to be in the hands of magical beings like you. I want more of us to feel free(r), to be able to make powerful choices for ourselves and our loved ones, to amplify the financial flow between creative, spiritual, witchy, weirdo women.

There, my secret's out!

And this is a huge part of my intention for writing this book. I want you to know YOUR book is just the beginning.

The potential around what it wants to be is limitless.

But before we get to the HOW, let's talk a bit more about what you (and those around you) might be expecting about what it means to be an Abundant Author.

Letting Go of Expectations

Let's get this out of the way to begin with:

I'm not a fan of the way most people talk about writing a book.

It's all 'become an international bestseller'.

Share your 'signature system'.

Strategy.

Status.

Numbers.

And all of these things can be important and valid.

But when I talk about becoming an Abundant Author, it's more than numbers. This process is about who you become as you write, publish and promote your book.

This process is about becoming more abundantly YOU.

And that might sound a bit fluffy. But, my friend, it's anything but. In fact, the very word 'abundant' can evoke feelings of candyfloss, unicorns, 'just recite this affirmation and put a happy face on it'. But in my experience, accessing the abundance that's inherently within you (so you get to experience more of it in your external circumstances) is so much more than that.

It's a ride.

And sometimes it's white knuckle.

That's what you're about to embark upon, magical one.

I'm all about ease and joy, but I can't guarantee that's all you'll experience as you read, implement and integrate what's within these pages. In fact, my clients tend to come to me for one thing and receive something completely different. #sorrynotsorry

So be prepared to be surprised.

And delighted.

The Abundant Author journey is pretty freaking epic. I'm excited for you.

Yes, there will be some strategy along the way. You'll definitely be invited to take action. I'm going to give you some steps that are, on the surface, pretty straightforward. But mostly... mostly this is about *who* you get to be.

Anyone can follow a step-by-step process – it's what you bring to it that's important. My invitation is for you to bring the most abundant expression of you along for the ride.

Are you ready?

Why am I so passionate about the idea of the Abundant Author?

Good question, magical one! I've been writing for years. And when I wrote my first book, *Heal Your Inner Good Girl*, I had this expectation that my life would transform as soon as it was released.

My business would take off.

The book would sell thousands of copies.

Tens, if not hundreds, more clients would come my way.

I'd have a chunky royalty cheque coming my way each month.

Whatever I offered in terms of courses, events or retreats would sell out immediately.

It was kinda like the feeling I described when I got my degree or passed my hypnotherapy training. Yet again, I thought I'd cracked it!

Oh dear, sweet, innocent 2016 Nicola.

I mean, it's totally possible for ALL of these things (and more) to happen when you publish a book.

I want this for you.

And also, the whole process of releasing a book and reaping the multi-faceted benefits is more nuanced than that.

I know it's a cliche, but as I mentioned earlier, writing a book is NOT a magic pill.

Well, it kinda IS. Because you can't help but be transformed by the process.

But also, it's not like winning the soul-led business lottery.

So, you may not magically transform into Louise Hay overnight.

Sorry to break that to you, hun.

And this is exactly why I'm so passionate about the idea of the Abundant Author. There's so much potential to be harvested from writing a book. It doesn't necessarily come automatically though. So this process is about becoming skilled at harvesting the gold.

I want you to become, receive, experience MORE as a result of your author journey.

As I said earlier, I want more magical, soul-led, heart-centred (whatever description floats your yacht) beings to be making bank. Because when big money gets into the hands of magical beings, the ripple effect is HUGE.

I want more spiritual entrepreneurs feeling beautifully financially supported as they do their thing and share their medicine with the world.

And of course, abundance isn't just about the money, honey. I know that. You know that. We're not JUST about the moolah. That's a given.

But it IS important.

We can make a huge positive impact AND make an abundant living.

The two aren't mutually exclusive.

In fact, they're very much linked.

A part of what I'll be inviting you to do with this process is getting to know and connecting with your vision; what's the change you want to create in the world? Because I know that absolutely you want to make more money (and it's SO okay to acknowledge that, magical soul), but you also want to make a difference.

So, you'll be getting up close and personal with that difference you want to make; getting to know it in all its specific glorious-ness. Because THAT's what's going to carry you through the challenging times and keep you going.

What is an author business?

That's a good question. Because it can all feel a bit serious; a bit (dare I say?) strategic; a bit 2013; a bit Amazon bestseller, Google ads, SEO, blah, blah, blah.

I don't want this to feel serious and/or heavy for you, magical soul. Because that doesn't feel abundant.

So what do I mean by author biz?

Well, it's simple really – what I mean is a business (i.e. a way of making money) that is based on your book.

It can be directly related to the content in your book, maybe a course, a mastermind, event, retreat or one-to-one work that takes your people through a process based on what you share in your book.

Or it can be indirectly related (i.e. a bit random or completely tenuous). For example, The Unbound Press was set up through me writing my second book, *UNBOUND*, but this business wasn't directly related to the content in that book. It was more 'inspired by'. I then went on to write *Unbound Writing*, which was actually directly related.

So perhaps your business or a particular offering is inspired by who you become (or are becoming) in the writing of your book?

Let me reiterate, what your author biz is NOT is focusing purely on book sales.

Book sales are great. We love the monthly royalty cheques that come our way. But there's SO much more potential than royalties alone. What you create based on your book is where the gold lies.

What are the ingredients of your Abundant Author business?

1) Your book! Of course. To be an author, you need a book. But it doesn't have to be written yet. You can start building your business before you've even written a word. And conversely it doesn't matter if your book has been out for YEARS. You get to bring it back to life through this process.

2) Embodiment. Please know this, how you BE in your business is as important as what you do. The energy you bring to each action is powerful. You can be doing all the 'right' things, but if something within you is constricted, it's going to feel off.

3) Visibility. A way to share who you are, what you do and how you can help your peeps. You already have a foundation for this with your book (and plenty of content therein). But you get to build on that in other ways.

4) An offer. You want to have something you offer in exchange for cash-a-roo. This could be a one-to-one service, a group program... you know the score. You probably have a range of ideas but for the purposes of this process, I recommend starting with one simple offer.

5) A way of sharing that offer with your people (and continuing to invite new people into your world who can connect with your work). In these pages we'll be focusing on the idea of 'laid-back launching'.

Before we move on, a quick note on 'embodiment'. I certainly don't want to give you the idea that you always have to be feeling amazing in your business. This is NOT about 'thinking positive' and slapping a happy face on everything.

You get to feel ALL the feelings. Yes the joyful, abundant, 'yes it's happening' ones AND also the 'wtf?', challenging, edgy ones.

The embodiment piece is all about how you relate to whatever you're experiencing and your feelings. Inhabiting your being as the Abundant Author you already are. And allowing yourself to be present with whatever's arising.

My aim with this book is to keep it simple. Super-simple.

There are SO many ways you could channel more abundance to you. That's a wonderful thing.

And it can also feel overwhelming.

So my Abundant Author process is designed to take the overwhelm away and give you focused, tangible steps to focus on.

I invite you to trust me as I guide you through these steps, uncovering a way that feels good to you and giving yourself at least three months to experiment with it.

A season of experimentation.

Invoking an energy of curiosity + play.

And seeing what happens...

How does that sound?

Abundance Miracle

As we begin, I want to ask you a powerful question;

What would feel like an abundance miracle to you right now?

This is a question I asked on an Abundant Author retreat day in the magical New Forest a while ago. I felt called to invite in the energy of the miraculous for the attendees. And now I invite you to do the same.

Because why not?

Why wouldn't you get to experience miracles?

Let's open the door to that as we start out on this journey together.

Take some time to feel into what YOUR abundance miracle might look like?

An expansion in your financial capacity.

A house by the ocean.

Selling out one of your offers.

Speaking on stage at a well-known event.

Feeling vibrant + full of radiant health.

Enjoying a loving relationship.

All of the above.

Don't limit yourself, magical one.

Let all of the details flow out freely onto the page.

Call in your heart's desires.

And be ready to notice the signs along the way that show the Universe is responding...

My abundance miracle looks/feels like...

The Concept that Changed Everything

One of the most transformational shifts I experienced in my business was the idea that it has a soul, essence, presence of its own, that my business is an energetic being which I get to co-create and collaborate with. It was Hiro Boga who introduced me to this via her Be Your Own Business Advisor program and it has been truly revolutionary for me.

Before that, I'd imagined that everything had to come from me; that I was the one who had to figure everything out. I sought help with this, listening to endless teleseminars, doing courses, reading books, and it felt very heady to me.

Heady and heavy.

I thought I had to figure everything out myself, that there was some previously hidden information that would unlock the door to success. I felt like I was missing something, lacking. And, of course, this is not a place of abundance.

In contrast, when Hiro guided me through a process to connect with the Deva of my business, I felt a lightness and spaciousness I'd never experienced around it. My business appeared to me as a golden book. At the time I took that as a message I needed to write a book. And as I was focusing on helping other women business owners with money mindset back then, I thought that's what the book should be about. Little did I know that I'd end up being a multiple author and founder of a publishing company!

My business has evolved so much since then, but knowing that it has an intelligence of its own has felt deeply reassuring.

This knowing has flowed into the way I approach and teach writing as well. One of the underlying principles of Unbound Writing is that your book has an energy, an essence, a spirit of its own. When you answer the call to write your book, you get to enter into a co-creative partnership with it. And that relationship doesn't end once the book makes its way into the world.

Like I said earlier, your book has its own blueprint – desires, intentions, a vision of its own. Its publication date is very much the beginning of its journey – the birth. From that point on, it gets to grow and flourish into what it's really here to be. And as the author, it's your job to support that process.

Are you up for that?

You may well have connected with your book in this way during the writing process, asking it what kind of ideas want to be expressed through it. But now I invite you to connect with your book to ask what it wants to become, what it wants to be the foundation for.

Connecting with the Vision of Your Book

Whatever stage you're at with your book, invite it into your awareness now.

Maybe you experience it visually, perhaps you hear it speaking to you, or you might have more of a felt sense of it connecting with you. Trust that however your book is connecting with you is perfect and enough.

As you come into relationship with your book, thank it for connecting with you. Let it know you're committed to helping it become all it wants to be in the world. You're excited to partner with it.

Notice how your book responds to this and how you feel to make this commitment.

Imagine that your book is a seed and you get to plant it in the fertile soil of Mother Earth.

Allow yourself to do this in the most tender and nurturing way. Feel the sacredness of this experience as you're supporting your book to flourish into its full potential.

As you plant the seed of your book, what happens?

What does it need to flourish?

As it starts to grow, ask it what it truly wants to become.

What is the most bountiful expression of your book's potential?

What vision is it here to fulfil?

Who and what does it want to come into connection with?

How does it want to support your people through what it grows into?

Take your time and notice what comes into awareness as you ask these questions. Answers may drop in immediately or over the next few hours and days.

Once you feel complete (and there's no rush, magical one), thank your book for connecting with you.

Allow yourself space to journal on what came through. You might like to go for a walk and let the insights your book gave you percolate and deepen.

Know that more and more clarity will drop in as you move through the Abundant Author process I'm guiding you through in these pages.

What insights did you gain from the Connecting with the Vision of Your Book process?

Embodiment & Intention

What is abundance?

Rather than diving straight into the strategy, how-tos and DOing, we're going to begin with BEing.

Who you are on your Abundant Author journey, what you believe, the energy you embody, how you show up and the intentions you hold, are key.

To help anchor into this, I invite you to get familiar with asking the question: *What does abundance mean to me?*

So often, or pretty much always, it's about more than money.

Yes, I want you to be and feel financially abundant. I want you to feel in a state of overflow when it comes to money. But abundance is a way of being that relates to all things.

Connection – with others, with ourselves, with nature.

Love. Joy. Peace, Health. Time. Space. Energy. Creativity. Courage.

Abundance is a generosity. A bounty. It's verdant, organic, unbridled, wild and free.

And you get to experience all of that. Not just in your relationship with money. But with all of life.

That's how we effect a real shift. In ourselves and our relationship with this planet.

More?

The definition of abundance in The Oxford Dictionary is:

> *existing or available in large quantities, plentiful.*

Existing or available in large quantities.

Plentiful.

How does it feel as you read those words?

To have an abundance of.

To BE an abundance of.

And there's a shift right here. Because often when we think about abundance, there's a focus on having, on getting and receiving more. But I want you to know that isn't necessarily the case.

Particularly in the online space, we're conditioned to always be going for more; more clients, more followers, more revenue, bigger teams, grow your presence, more, more, more.

And if that feels truly abundant, all power to you. The intention of the Abundant Author journey is for more magical writers to be receiving more of life's good stuff.

But there's something to be said for the abundant appreciation of what's already there. Yes, growing your audience, client base, revenue, presence, but to a place that feels sustainable. And kind. To you. And others.

Abundance is a quality. A felt sense. It's not about numbers. There's a richness to it. Something organic.

In continually striving for more, it's easy to lose that. We can end up pushing, trying, thinking we have to bend ourselves into shapes to get more.

So, how about shifting the focus and allowing yourself to BE an abundance of who you're here to be?

How about being an abundance of YOU?

Allowing a plentiful supply of YOU-ness to flow into the world.

How does that feel?

When we shift the focus in this way, we move our attention from the external and 'trying to make things happen', to the internal.

We get to radiate the energy of abundance.

We get to embody it.

And The Universe can't help but respond to that.

Now, I'm not talking about just sitting back and not taking action. (Although seasons of BEing can be just as, if not more, powerful than seasons of DOing.) We want to have a balance between being abundant and taking the inspired action we feel called to take from that place. And that's what we'll be exploring in these very pages.

It's always powerful to ask yourself the question:

How can I be myself more plentifully in this situation?

Whether that's when you're showing up being visible and connecting with others, creating offers, launching something new, writing your book or going about your daily life.

How can I be myself more plentifully?

How can I invite more of myself forward?

Notice how these questions feel in your body. Do you feel a sense of expansion or opening? Or are you aware of something contracting, closing down?

If you do, then be curious.

Notice where you experience any contraction in your body and move your attention to that place. Ask the question, *What do you want me to know about this?*

See what bubbles up and follow that thread.

There's very likely to be fear around being yourself more fully. Often we've been criticised, scolded, shut down for being too full of ourselves.

Historically women have been shamed, abused or killed for expressing themselves. So the invitation to be yourself more plentifully can feel edgy, risky, downright dangerous.

You get to go at your own pace here, magical one.

This isn't about being all RAHHHHH! and roaring into the world (although that might be exactly what you feel called to).

Subtle shifts can make a big difference here.

If you feel called to go gently, do that.

A little bit more YOU every day.

We'll be diving into this some more when we get to the Visibility section, but for now, I invite you to begin by tuning into what abundance means to YOU. Because it will mean something different to each person. And the way you relate to it will shift and evolve at different times.

Let's uncover what abundance is for you right now...

Take some time to journal on these prompts:

What does the energy of abundance feel like to me?

How does abundance feel in my body?

When have I felt most abundant? Is there a particular time in your life when you felt especially abundant? What was happening? Who were you with? What was most present in your life at that time? What were you doing, being and having?

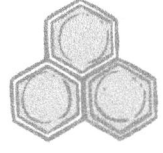

Abundance is...

I know I'm abundant when...

Think of a person who feels abundant to you. What in particular about them expresses the energy of abundance?

Abundance is not...

Describe your most abundant day. Imagine waking up in the morning and feeling completely abundant — what would you do? What would you NOT do? What would you wear? What would you eat? Where would you be? Who would you be with?

If I felt truly abundant in my business, I would...

If I felt truly abundant in my life, I would...

Some of these prompts may resonate more than others. Allow yourself to explore them all and be curious about what comes through. The idea is to get familiar with the energy of abundance so that as you move through the process ahead, you'll KNOW when you're in it.

Connecting with Your Inner Abundant Author

A process I invite you to do as you begin this journey is connecting with your Inner Abundant Author.

Maybe you don't identify with being an author right now?

And perhaps you don't identify with being abundant?

But I want you to know that if you've been drawn to this book, you most certainly have the qualities of an Abundant Author within you. So, let's connect with that energy that's already there.

The first step is to find somewhere you won't be disturbed. Make yourself comfortable and close your eyes (if that feels good). *Obviously you'll want to read through these instructions before you do that.*

Take a few deep breaths.

Then invite the Abundant Author you are into your presence.

You might experience this visually, seeing an image of yourself as an Abundant Author.

You might have a felt sense of that quality within you.

You might hear words or phrases from your Inner Abundant Author.

Be open and curious.

Allow your Abundant Author to connect with you and trust that however that happens is just the way it's meant to be.

Notice how it feels to connect with that energy within you, to know that it's already present. You don't need to force it. Allow.

Please know it may take a few times to feel a strong connection. This is a practice and we're simply opening the doors to your Abundant Author right now. The relationship will strengthen and evolve over time.

But for now simply ask the question, what do I need to know?

And see what comes.

Maybe you'll receive a message of support, perhaps you'll receive some guidance or a clue towards your next steps.

Again, there's no 'right way' here. Even if you simply feel some kind of connection, however tenuous, it's all good. As you read this book and experiment with some of the suggestions in it, you'll develop a closer relationship with the Abundant Author you already are.

You can access an MP3 of the Connecting with Your Inner Abundant Author meditation at: <ins>nicolahumber.com/abundant-author-resources</ins>

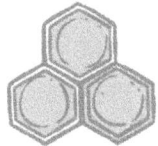

Beliefs & Stories

As we start from a place of Embodiment and Intention, it's time to acknowledge any fears, doubts or old restrictive stories that have been bubbling up for you.

The idea of abundance, particularly financial abundance, can be a huge trigger for many of us spiritually aligned humans. I'm pretty sure you've done a freak ton of work around your money mindset, uncovering and clearing limiting beliefs, looking at where constrictive patterns were formed, maybe even revisiting past lives to discover what might be impacting you from before this lifetime.

I remember when I first started running my own business and discovered money mindset was a thing, it felt like a full-time job! There was so much 'stuff' I felt I had to clear before I could actually start making good money. And I'm grateful for all the work I did, everything I uncovered, the awareness I gained. BUT I made myself wrong, SO many times.

It took ages for me to realise there wasn't actually something seriously amiss with me, I wasn't broken, and that I could access financial abundance without having to clear every last limiting belief or pattern.

And that's what I want you to know as we're setting out here:

You can have fears, doubts, limiting beliefs, patterns around scarcity and lack AND still create financial abundance.

You get to receive more money exactly as you are right now.

Yes, it's helpful to have an awareness of your patterns.

And you'll get to gain more awareness as you move through the Abundant Author process.

But you don't have to change who you are.

Abundance is here for you now.

You just have to stop making yourself wrong.

The first step towards that is not just to acknowledge any fears, doubts or stories that are bubbling up as you begin this journey, but to WELCOME them.

You might be thinking, 'What?? Nicola, I just want to push all of this stuff as far away as possible!'

And I get that.

But the truth is as an Abundant Author you get to be abundantly YOU – the fullest, freest expression of who you're here to be in the world. And that doesn't mean only allowing the parts of you that are shiny and positive. The dark, limiting, fearful, doubting parts of you get to be expressed too. (In fact, often when you feel more comfortable sharing these parts of yourself, it creates a deeper sense of connection with your people.)

Just as with the Unbound Writing process, you get to transmute ALL parts of your experience into the gold of compelling connection.

You get to welcome ALL of you into this process.

And awareness is the first step to alchemising any 'stuff' that's coming to the surface.

So, how does this work exactly?

Well, you want to acknowledge anything you've previously pushed away into the shadows: the 'I'm not good enough', 'Abundance isn't for people like me', 'To make more money I'd have to work really hard' fears, doubts and restrictive stories.

We bring them out into the open and simply acknowledge them as a completely normal part of being a human being who is expanding into her multi-faceted, most magnificent, Unbound Self. (Believe me, EVERYONE experiences the same kind of fears and doubts when it comes to sharing their magic with the world.)

This simple acknowledgement is the first step to moving beyond your 'stuff'.

Take some time to ask the question: What are the thoughts, feelings and stories that have been making me believe it's not possible for me to create abundance in my life?

Write down whatever comes up, without censoring yourself or trying to justify what bubbles up. I'm sure a lot (if not all) that comes up won't necessarily be new to you. You may have worked with these beliefs MANY times. Even if it's one of your old familiars, write it down. It's easy to beat ourselves up and/or not want to acknowledge a fear or doubt because we feel we should be over it already. That's not the vibe here. I want you to cultivate a sense of acceptance and empowerment. And that begins with being clear with and making space for what's present.

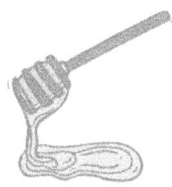

Give yourself at least 10 minutes for this. Whenever you feel yourself stopping, ask the question, 'And what else?'

When you've done this, take some time to look at what you've written. Aim for an attitude of playful curiosity as you do this.

Know that you don't have to do anything else right now to shift or release these fears and doubts. Bringing them to the surface is powerful in itself.

How do you feel to allow space for these thoughts and feelings that maybe you've tried to push away in the past?

The Abundant Author Audit

Now you've tuned into what abundance means to you, connected with your inner Abundant Author and got up close and personal with any fears or doubts that are bubbling up, I invite you to take stock.

I'm all about visioning into a magical future, but what about the magic that's already here? Right now. Under your feet in the fertile soil of the life you've already created. Can you feel the potential waiting to burst through? I can. It's palpable.

So, let's take some time uncovering and acknowledging what is. Whether it feels like you're aeons away from where you want to be or right on track, there's no judgement here, no right or wrong. There's simply what is.

The invitation is to reflect on the following questions from a place of curiosity. You may not have an answer to all of them (yet). That's perfect. We're gathering intel for what's to come, signs, clues. Who knows what might bubble up as you take this time to reflect?

Shall we?

What is the focus of your book(s)?

What do you feel passionate about right now?

What did you love doing as a child?

What did you dream of becoming when you were little?

If you already have a business, what do you help people with?

What offerings do you currently have?

Do they feel aligned with what's coming through in your writing? If not, why not?

How do you most enjoy working with people — online, in-person, one-to-one, groups? Long-term, short-term, intensive?

What ideas do you currently have around an offering/offerings you could create around your book?

What does your book want to become?

What's the vision you hold for your book? For yourself? For your readers?

What journey do you want to take people on?

If you had to describe who you are, what would you say?

What 3-5 qualities do you want to experience as you go on your Abundant Author journey?

What's the change you want to see in the world?

What challenges have you overcome?

How do you feel about visibility?

What platforms do you prefer for sharing your message?

How do you like to connect with people?

How do you feel about the pricing of any current offers you have?

If you were going to do a TED Talk, what would it be about?

After you've answered these questions, give yourself some space. You might head out for a walk, get yourself some lunch or sleep on your Abundant Author Audit. Take as long as you feel you need to let your answers percolate. (That might be an hour or it could be a few days.)

When you feel ready, come back to them and ask yourself:

What's my number one learning here?

What feels good about what's already in place?

What feels challenging about what's already there?

This will put you in good stead for our next section where we're going to set some intentions.

Setting Intentions for Your Onward Journey

So, magical one, we've begun! In this section we've been diving into how to embody the Abundant Author you are more fully.

How do you feel about moving forward?

Now that you've begun to lay some powerful foundations – go you! – I invite you to set some intentions about what comes next.

Taking even a few minutes now to tune into how you want to feel, what you want to experience and what you desire to create as you set sail on your Abundant Author journey will put you in good stead.

I'm sure I don't need to tell you about how powerful it is to set intentions. Giving your subconscious mind some direction, letting the big U know more about what you want and inviting in support from your guides, known and unknown, will set in motion an energetic shift, clearing the way for MORE to come to you.

I recommend you set intentions on three levels: what you want to experience personally, what you want your clients to experience, and the impact you want your work to have on the collective. You're here to activate transformation and that will ripple out into all parts of both your individual field and the collective.

It's time to acknowledge and channel your potency!

Shall we?

Grab your journal + take some time to reflect on the following questions:

Individual Intentions:

How do I want to feel as I step more fully into the Abundant Author I'm here to be? What qualities do I want to experience more of?

What do I want to open to?

Who am I becoming as I embark on this journey?

What do I want to create?

How do I want to create?

Who and/or what might support me as I move forwards?

Your Clients

What do you want those who connect with your work to experience?

How do you want them to feel as they come into contact with your work?

What kind of people do you desire to work with?

What's the transformation you want to hold space for?

The Collective

What's the change you're here to make?

What impact do you want your work to have on the world?

What energy/qualities are you sending out into the collective?

Vibrant Visibility

Vibrant Visibility – The Art of Connection

Ah, visibility. This piece of the Abundant Author puzzle can send us sensitive souls into a tailspin.

You need to be seen in order to reach the people your work is for. You know that. But there's a part of you that would much prefer to remain invisible.

This is where so many authors struggle. The conflict between wanting to be seen by more people and not wanting to be seen at all is ongoing. But the thing is you've written or are writing a book. The intention for that is obviously for it to be read by (hopefully many!) people. If that's not visibility, I don't know what is.

Can you let yourself be seen, magical one?

There are a few issues that can bubble up here:

1) The desire to fly under the radar. 'Can't my book and my work reach the people it's meant to without me having to be more visible?'

2) Confusion over how to be visible. 'There are SO many platforms! Which should I choose? And how should I share? Writing, video, audio??'

3) Resistance to social media. 'It's all so distracting and overwhelming. I don't want to have to create this perfect persona like everyone else!'

If you're feeling any of the above (or all of them), you're not alone. And it's okay, my friend. I've got you.

There are ways to reach more people without having to be online 24/7 or slipping into misalignment. You get to be you. You get to find a way that feels good. You get to do it your way.

Honestly, since I began my own business back in 2010, I think I've experimented with EVERYTHING when it comes to visibility. I started with blogging. (A very dry and professional blog to begin with that had very little me in it.) Then I began to play with social media, Facebook at first, with a dash of YouTube. You can go back and see my first videos when I still had a hypnotherapy practice and was helping women with weight loss. Actually, don't, they're a total cringefest!

But that's the point, everyone has to start somewhere. We're all in process with this stuff. Even the most successful authors and spiritual entrepreneurs began their visibility journey tentatively (and probably with a big helping of cringe!) No one gets this stuff right off the bat.

For me, it's been a 14+ year journey of trying things out. Instagram, Periscope (remember that?), Twitter (not for me), LinkedIn (also not really for me), TikTok, podcasting, writing articles, appearing on summits and creating my own. I've always given myself permission to experiment and see what happens.

And that's what I'll be inviting you to do in this section.

But let's go step by step. And let's begin by reframing what visibility is.

Visibility/Connection

Rather than thinking of visibility, which can feel one-dimensional and focused purely on how you look, what if you shifted perspective to think of it as connection?

In your work as an Abundant Author, you want to connect with more people, more deeply.

So rather than asking the question, *Am I willing to be seen?* can you shift it to, *Am I willing to be felt? Am I willing to be in connection?*

How does that feel?

Because this is the key:

Connection.

Every. Single. Time.

Connection with yourself. Connection with what you're here to do. Connection with others.

That's what's gonna activate abundance.

And it's a process.

Unearthing the treasure, the gifts.

If you can carve out time each day to cultivate connection, you're winning. Especially in a world that pretty much conditions us to disconnect. The constant urge to scroll, to numb, to distract. Oh, my goddess, it's addictive.

And you certainly don't want to judge yourself for disconnecting. I'm sharing that because I do it all the time. I used to berate myself for it. Why couldn't I stop the scroll? That unconscious urge to pick up my phone, or the desire to put the latest Netflix crush on. *Selling Sunset*, anyone?

But then I thought, what if I could have some compassion here?

What if I could accept this part of me?

What if I could actually move into deep agreement with the urge to disconnect, to numb out, to switch off?

And conversely I felt more connected. Ha!

That's how the magic works. Compassion over judgement. Allowing over trying.

This is what's going to serve you well on your visibility journey. And when you shift your focus to connection, your people will feel it.

Be Abundantly YOU

As we begin this stage of the journey, can I ask you a question, magical one?

Are you allowing yourself to be fully you?

If you're not, I get it. The world we live in is not at all set up for those in marginalised groups to feel safe being fully expressed. That's why I felt called to my work around being unbound. It's not a simple process and there's no end point. I'm certainly not completely unbound, I'm unbinding. And I'm sure that's the case for you too.

We're conditioned to hold back and keep ourselves small (or certainly smaller than the limitless beings we truly are).

We're taught that it's safer to shrink, to keep parts of us hidden, to rein our magic in.

Don't stand out.

Stick with the crowd.

Dull your shine.

And whatever you do, NEVER get too big for your boots!

Well my friend, when it comes to being visible, when it comes to connecting more deeply with your people and allowing yourself to be seen, heard, felt, I'm going to invite you to turn this on its head.

The underlying premise here is:

In order to access (more) abundance, you need to (get to) be an abundance of you.

Be Full of Yourself

I used to have a couple of friends who would often describe others as being 'full of themselves' when they met someone new who seemed especially confident.

'Yeah, he was nice, but he was kinda full of himself.'

Or, *'She does a great job, but she's really full of herself.'*

It used to trigger me, but I got it. Because as I talked about above, this is exactly what we've been conditioned to do: rein it in, pipe down and don't be a show-off.

So when we see others popping their heads even slightly above the parapet, it can feel unsafe.

Danger, danger! Someone's being a little too 'more than…'. I need to shut this down and judging them as being 'too full of themselves' is a way to do that.

They're getting it wrong. And me over here hiding my proverbial light under a bushel? I'm most definitely getting it right.

What I never asked my friends (and I wish I had) is: wtf else would we want to be other than full of ourselves?

I personally don't want to be full of anything or anyone else, apart from my magnificent, Unbound Self.

And I want the same for YOU & everyone else.

I'm tired of living in a world where being fully expressed is seen as a BAD thing, something to be judged, shamed and reined the fuck in.

And for the purposes of the Abundant Author process, your people are only going to recognise and come into connection with you if they can see/hear/feel who you truly are.

So I invite you to reflect on these questions now:

What would it feel like if I gave myself permission to be full of myself?

What would I do/express differently?

How would I show up online and in person?

How would I choose to share my magic and what would I choose to share?

Invoking the Magic of 'Too Much'

Ah, the old 'too much' piece.

Have you ever battled with the idea that you're simultaneously too much and not enough? If the answer's yes, you're not alone.

Particularly as women, the Patriarchy LOVES to place us in this pickle. One minute you're judging yourself for holding back and not being able to make your mark, the next you're feeling shamed for unleashing your magic and expressing yourself more freely.

It's a conundrum that has no straightforward answer. I mean, I'm all for dismantling the Patriarchy. Our books and the body of work we create around them is absolutely a way we're doing that. But in the meantime, we need to access more of our full-ness (and feel at least kinda okay with that).

Yes, there will be people who judge you as 'too much'. They are not your people. And I realise that's probably not at all reassuring.

Again as women we've been conditioned to please. Knowingly going against that takes courage. I've personally had to become (more) comfortable with irritating/disappointing/pissing people off. As a recovering good girl, I don't find it easy at ALL. But the alternative – squeezing my magic back into its box – is just not an option at this point.

Your people will revel in your too-muchness. It will give them hope. It will give them permission to express themselves more freely. It will connect them with their own magic. And it will draw them closer to you.

They may well feel uncomfortable or triggered by what you share and how you share it. But that's okay.

On stage at coach Suzy Ashworth's Quantum Leap event, when she asked how I first connected and came to work with her, I had to admit that I'd chosen to unfollow her for a number of years. Her unabashed approach had initially drawn me in and then repelled me. It took me a long time to tentatively come back into connection with her. And when I finally did, I quickly joined one of her year-long transformational programs, ending up on the success panel at her in-person event.

This is how it can roll. And it's important not to take it personally when someone unfollows you, stops being a client or ghosts you.

I've had clients I've worked with for years unfollow and unsubscribe.

I've had people come into my world in a blaze of 'Oh my goddess, I LOVE your work!', downloading every freebie, commenting on all of my posts, buying my offerings and then disappearing without a trace.

Everyone is in their own process.

Taking it personally is not the way.

The important thing we get to do as the Abundant Authors we are is to keep showing up and being our full, too-much selves.

On that note...

Freakishly Potent

These words came through in my journaling as I was writing this section of the book:

'Let your words be freakishly potent.'

What does that mean?

Well, the truth is many of us have felt like freaks for some (*if not al*l) our lives. Not quite fitting in, being the odd one out, kinda weird.

And when it comes to being an Abundant Author – being full of yourself, invoking your too-muchness, bringing an abundance of YOU into how you share your magic – we get to wave our freak flags.

We get to bring our weird, our quirks and so-called imperfections into everything we do.

Unbound Writer Jennifer Mayol has the most incredible oracle card deck – *Strange Grace* – and one of the cards is Odd Creatures. A line in the message of the card declares:

'Here I am, standing with dignity, strong in my strangeness and quirk.'

Can you feel that?

Can you allow yourself to stand strong in your own strangeness and quirk?

What does that feel like?

This is the vibe I'm inviting you into in this section. All of us Odd Creatures together.

Connecting with Your People Meditation

We get to experience more of our own inherent abundance and the external expression of that through connection. When we connect with others, there's the potential to have our innate abundance reflected back to us (and do the same for those we're connecting with). It's a magical thing.

As we've been talking about, the beginning point for the Abundant Author journey will always be connection.

Connection with ourselves.

Connection with others.

A simple way to do this, before we even start taking any kind of action, especially around visibility, is with a simple meditation. I hesitate to use the word meditation as it can make us feel heady. But this is very much about being and experiencing a felt sense of connection.

The first step is to close your eyes, make yourself comfortable and breathe.

Take a few moments or minutes to settle into a feeling of presence.

As you do that, set the intention to experience an awareness of the people you're here to connect with, those who will read your book and be attracted to your work.

You might see them visually.

You might have a felt sense of them.

Trust that your intention to connect with them is enough.

As you become aware of your people, bring your attention to your heart space. Allow yourself to experience a sense of opening there, an abundance of heart energy.

As you feel your heart open, imagine you're connecting with the hearts of each of the other beings you're here to inspire and support in some way.

Feel a sense of love and abundance flowing between you.

Enjoy that feeling as long as you'd like to.

As you connect with your people, ask the questions:

What do you want to hear or see from me right now?

What would serve you most powerfully?

How do you want me to connect with you?

What do you need to know in order to take the next step?

Notice what comes into your awareness as you ask these questions. You want to remain in a feeling, rather than a thinking place here. Allow what wants to come – some days there may be a stream of insight, other days there might be nothing.

Know that connecting with your people in the energetic field in this way can't help but bring them closer to you in the physical world.

You may like to experiment with this as a daily practice and/or spend a few minutes connecting in this way before sharing anything related to your work or writing.

Trust and act on any specific inspiration that comes through this process.

What insights came through for you during this meditation?

You can access an MP3 of the Connecting with Your People meditation at: nicolahumber.com/abundant-author-resources

Pick Your Platforms

Too many magical women I know feel overwhelmed with the idea of visibility because there are SO many ways to do it.

Which social media platform should I focus on?

What about a podcast?

Should I start a blog or a Substack?

Is it best to use video, audio or writing?

Oh, man! This feels like it could be a full-time job.

And the truth is, it could. There have been many seasons in my business when I spent most of my time creating content (with very little benefit in terms of new clients or cash flow). I don't want that for you.

The key is to be discerning.

You don't need to do ALL the things to connect with your people. You get to pick the most potent platforms for you. In my personal experience and observing what works for others, it's best to go all in with a couple, rather than spreading yourself too thinly.

And it doesn't all have to happen online. Maybe you prefer to focus on in-person connection, through events (your own and other peoples') or networking? I often have to remind the writers I work with (and myself!) that people had businesses before social media!

Take a look at the list below and notice which 2-3 platforms feel most aligned to you, your work and your people:

Facebook	Blogging	Email
Instagram	YouTube	Magazines
LinkedIn	Podcast	Events
TikTok	Summits	Public speaking
Substack	Articles	Networking – online
Twitter/X	Pinterest	Networking – in-person

Wow, there's a lot there, eh? And rather than seeing that as overwhelming, what if you could feel the magical possibilities of having an abundance of ways to connect? What a time to be alive when we get to connect in so many different ways – a way for everyone.

Which resonate with you most deeply?

Which do you feel will resonate with your people?

Honestly, you can't get this wrong. Go with your initial feelings.

For me, right now as I'm writing this (and it might have changed by the time you're reading it!), here's my visibility recipe:

Email is the foundation. I write a Sunday love note to my peeps every week, pretty much without fail.

Instagram is my social media platform of choice. I use stories, Reels and written posts.

Facebook is the place for community – both for my paid offerings and a free group.

And finally we have The Unbound Writer's Club podcast which goes out every week. This helps to create content for the other platforms – email and social media.

I do other things along the way – sometimes speaking at events, online and in-person, being a guest on podcasts – but those four core ingredients above are what really push the needle for me when it comes to visibility.

So, how about you? What are you going to put in your mix?

For the purposes of this process, pick one core platform and 2-3 others to experiment with. Know you get to shift and change your mind later. But let's give them at least three months to begin with.

Write them below:

My core platform for connection will be:

_____

My secondary platforms are:

_____

_____

_____

Now, let's harness the power of what you already have to share your magic...

Optimise & Harvest

Okay, my love, what we're going to do first is lay the foundations for abundance and make it super-easy for people to know:

1) Who you are

2) What you do

3) How they can connect and work with you.

Of course, if your book is already out there, then they may be coming to you after reading that. They'll already have a good sense of who you are, but they may not know how to go deeper.

And if someone's completely new to you, then you want to make it clear what their next steps may be.

The simplest way to do this is to make sure your bio on social media platforms is up-to-date and focused. Whatever platforms you're using, there will be a place where you get to share a little about who you are and what you do.

Often it's going to be a super-short space, so you want to be discerning about what you share there. I'm all for a bit of fluff when it comes to writing (you might have noticed!), but our bios need to be concise.

The good news is you can change them up regularly. But whatever your focus is right now – whether that's talking about your book, a freebie or a particular offering – that's what you want to include in your bio.

I don't want you to overthink this. The invitation here is to take a look at your bio on any platform you use (particularly the core one you've chosen) and make sure it's doing what it's meant to do.

Let me give you an example. Here's my current bio on Instagram:

Nicola Humber – Transformational Writing Mentor + Publisher *(Says what I do clearly and also mentions the 'transformational' – aka non-basic – nature of my work.)*

Rebel leader of The Unbound Press *(Our PR Magician at The Unbound Press, Sarah Lloyd, gave me this title and I'm claiming it! 'Rebel leader' has more personality than 'founder' and suggests that The Unbound Press is a movement rather than just a publishing company.)*

Let's get your book written in 2024 (because it's needed!) *(As I'm writing this it's January 2024 and those beginning-of-the-year vibes are strong, so I'm acknowledging that and letting people know I can help them to write their book if that's one of their goals.)*

Doors now open to Birth Your Transformational Book *(This is my main current offer, so I'm sign-posting people to that.)*

Then I have my link which highlights not only BYTB, but my membership and free book-writing guide, so there's something for everyone, whether they want to dip a toe or dive right in. I use LinkTree for this, but you can absolutely set up a page on your website with different links.

I'm definitely not saying my Insta bio is perfect, but it does the job.

On Facebook, you have less room to play with. Here's what I say:

'Helping magical beings write + publish world-changing books.'

Short and sweet with a link to my free book-writing guide.

So, over to you. I invite you to head over to the bio section on the social media platforms you've chosen to focus on and tweak them. Make sure they're up-to-date and clear about how you can help your people.

This isn't something to set and forget.

I recommend checking in with your bio once a month to give it a refresh. And I'm going to remind you again NOT to overthink this! Honestly there's something about trying to distil our magic into a bio that prompts many unbound beings to freeze. Because of course it's impossible to express everything about who you are and what you do in relatively few words. So, remember, that's not the intention. You just want to give people enough to go on, a taste of who you are and a way to connect more deeply with you.

You can't get this wrong.

Heartstorm your bio here:

What to share?

So, now the foundations are in place, what do you share?

I'm sure you've been sharing at least bits and pieces already. But the thing I see most authors missing is that they already have a freak ton of content right under their nose (their books), but instead keep thinking they have to reinvent the wheel. I'm totally outing myself here, btw.

So, please remember you can be dipping into that for much of what you share.

However you're choosing to connect and be visible, your content will hold at least one, and ideally more, of these three energies:

Intimacy – sharing your story, a snippet of your personal experience which helps your people to come closer and get to know you better.

Inspiration – content that gives them a sense of what's possible.

Information – sharing helpful tips and guidance your people can use to move forward right away.

If you can, it's powerful to include all three of these in one share. You certainly want to make sure you're sprinkling in all the elements.

Let me give you an example. This is a post I shared on Insta and Facebook as I was bringing together the manuscript for this very book:

> *We never know when clarity will drop in.*
>
> *Right now we're in the middle of a month-long writing sprint in The Unbound Writer's Club membership. The invitation has been to show up for your book for at least 5 minutes a day. And after the first week or so, I've been struggling to find the enthusiasm.*

I've written quite a bit for my next book – The Abundant Author – but I've got to a point where I wasn't quite sure how to move forward. So, I've been flossing around the edges, moving pieces from here to there, trying to create more flow and structure. And then...

...yesterday after another few minutes of flossing, I was in the bath with a glass of wine   And all of a sudden a shiz-load of clarity landed.

I immediately knew what the book REALLY wanted to be and how it related to the new Abundant Author Academy that's coming in the Spring. It's SO much simpler than I imagined it could be (and so much more powerful).

We never know when clarity is going to land.

And often right before it does are the times when we feel most frustrated + uncertain. The key is to sit with that.

Rather than rushing to know and trying to force the clarity. Let yourself sit with the not knowing.

Because you never know what's on the other side, magical one...

Okay, so in this post I'm sharing a story. It's not a big, life-changing story, but it mirrors something I'm sure my people will be familiar with – losing momentum with their writing.

By sharing this personal experience, I'm creating connection through *Intimacy*. An added bonus is that I'm very naturally sharing about three of my offerings:

The Unbound Writer's Club membership
This book
The Abundant Author Academy

Through the story, I'm creating *Inspiration* – you never know when clarity will land. It could happen at any moment, when you least expect it.

And I end with a dash of *Information* and giving the reader some guidance – let yourself sit with the not knowing.

It's a relatively short post, but it covers each of the bases. And tbh, I didn't sit down to write something that included Intimacy + Inspiration + Information. It happened quite naturally. And that's how it gets to be for you too.

Here are some prompts to help spark you off. They're heavy on the Intimacy (story-based), as this is what's going to make what you're sharing unique. Even if you just give a line or two providing some context of a personal experience, whatever Inspiration/Information you share afterwards will land more fully.

Intimacy

Tell the story of:

1) Where did it all begin for you?
2) Why you feel called to the work you're doing now
3) A struggle you've overcome
4) A breakthrough moment
5) Someone who's supported you on your journey
6) Someone who challenged you on your journey
7) The best advice you ever received
8) The worst advice you ever received
9) A major turning point
10) Something you didn't expect
11) What it was like when you started out
12) Something that's happened over the past week or so that helped you see things differently
13) A fuck-it moment, when you decided to take a different path
14) Something that scares you
15) The story that feels super-edgy to share
16) Something that happened today that relates to your work
17) A secret dream or seemingly impossible hope you hold

18) An experience that inspired you

19) A lesson you learned recently

20) A lesson you learned way back

21) Something you kept hidden for a long time

22) A time you felt lost (and how you found your way)

23) A time you went deeper

24) How a mentor changed your perspective

25) An experience of saying 'No'

26) An experience of saying 'Yes'

27) A moment of inspiration

28) Something that felt like a miracle at the time

29) A dark night of the soul

30) Something hilarious

31) A time you thought you'd screwed up

32) Something you thought was true and then realised it wasn't

33) What supports you

Inspiration

34) Write a manifesto where you share your values, hopes and dreams for people you're here to work with.

35) What do you feel most passionate about right now? What do you want people to know about this subject?

36) Share something around what your clients experience when working with you. What shifts do they experience?

37) What's the change you want to see in the world?

38) What's your vision/mission?

39) What do your people want to experience differently?

40) What's the shadow side of your work? Whatever field/area you are focusing on, talk to what's being kept in the shadows in this area. What's unspoken about this topic?

41) What might be hidden in the shadows for your people. Where might they be experiencing resistance around the subject you're writing about? What might they have pushed away or suppressed? What might they have forgotten about themselves in relation to this subject?

Information

42) Give a tip advising your people how to move through resistance they might be experiencing.

43) What areas can you provide guidance around? Come up with three tips for each area.

44) Share five tips to support your reader with a specific challenge.

45) What one thing could your people do today to move forward?

46) Advice for creating a breakthrough

47) A tool or practice that could support your audience

48) A how-to guide around one area of your work

49) A simple tip they could use immediately

50) A guide to recommended resources

Remember, you want to share content that encapsulates each of these energies.

Intimacy creates connection.

Inspiration expands perspective.

Information enables action.

Just knowing this can help when it comes to the question of what the freak to post!

Take a moment now to write down a list of possible content you could create in each area. I'm going to say it again – you'll get tired of this! But... – Don't. Overthink. It.

You might respond, 'But Nicola, what about quality over quantity?' And I have something to say around that...

Quantity vs Quality

There's a general agreement that we should focus on quality over quantity when it comes to... well, just about anything really.

But when it comes to visibility, this can mess with us. I mean, it seems to make sense. Of course you want to share quality content. You don't want to be putting stuff out there for the sake of it.

But what does 'quality' actually mean? We can get up into our heads about this, questioning whether that post we've written or that video we've created is 'quality' enough. What if it's a bit average? Should we still share it? Or should we wait for our genius to strike?

Before we know it, days (or weeks) have gone by and we haven't shared a thing because we've been waiting for that elusive quality to drop in.

When it comes to being visible, what I know to be true is that familiarity creates connection. I know the word 'consistency' can trigger us unbound types, but we benefit from showing up in a dedicated way for our people, even when we're not feeling 100% inspired.

I can pretty much guarantee that even when you're feeling a bit meh and the post you're writing falls flat for you, someone will see it and feel seen/be inspired/want to come closer to you and your work.

Conversely (and I know this from hard experience!) that post you've written that feels SO potent and completely on point may well fly under the radar and get no engagement at all.

Sorry to break it to you, magical one, but we're just not the best judge of what's 'quality' when it comes to our own content.

And actually that's a brilliant thing.

Because you get to let go of any expectation to produce 'the best thing ever' with every single piece of content you share and know that whatever you create is good enough. Honestly, it is.

This is why I'm such a fan of having a daily sharing practice. In 2022, I started doing this with my #unbound365 share on Instagram. I stopped when I went on retreat in June of that year, but I still pretty much share at least one post (and usually stories) every day.

When we do this, we move from a place of asking:

Am I going to share something today?

To:

What will I share today?

It might seem counterintuitive but this takes the pressure WAY off. Because rather than waiting until you have something mind-blowing to share, you get to put something out there every day.

For more on this, I recommend checking out Simone Grace Seol's Garbage Post Challenge. Just google it and her podcast episode about it will come up.

Let your people get to know you. Show up for them regularly – if not daily then a few times a week.

That connection can't help but activate abundance.

Your people want to see YOU.

They want to get to know you, not just the wisdom you have to share, but the details of your everyday life.

You might not believe that. I know I didn't for a very long time.

I was comfortable sharing information and even life events + circumstances that directly related to my work. But anything else made me feel like a twonk.

I always say that your story is what will bring your book to life. But sharing ourselves can feel edgy.

The whole 'too much' piece I talked about earlier can rear its judgemental head.

This only shifted for me when I started to notice the content I most enjoyed online. Yes, I'm here for learning from others, watching and reading informational content. Bring it on.

But the posts and stories that really draw me in tend to be those where someone is sharing their everyday life; what they get up to around and in between their work.

The trips they're going on, the restaurants they're headed to, the relationship they have with their partner, kids or pets.

I'm a sucker for the seemingly small details.

You could call me nosey.

And I'm guessing most people are.

We want to get to know those we follow in all their different layers. Not just what they have to teach us, but who they are as a human being.

It helps to build a sense of connection and trust.

This is another layer of the Intimacy content I mentioned earlier in this section.

When I realised that's the kind of content I craved myself, I started to become more comfortable sharing it myself.

And it doesn't even have to be directly relevant to your work. There doesn't always need to be a learning point. You can share, just as you would with a friend.

The truth is, some people who follow me will be switched off by it. When I'm sharing my experiment with two-hour daily walks around my home town or Mr H's and my latest kitchen disco, there will be some who feel repelled and hit the unfollow button.

And that's okay. Because there will be others who come closer, who feel more connected with me and want to journey onwards.

So, as part of the invitation around Visibility, I encourage you to experiment with sharing more of your everyday. Taking your people behind the scenes, even if it feels irrelevant and frivolous.

Your Invitation

Okay magical one, so as you've read through this section you should be clear(er) on:

The purpose of visibility – to create and deepen connection

How you want to share – your one core platform and 2-3 secondary ones

What you want to share – a blend of Intimacy, Inspiration and Information content.

Now I want you to put this all together into your own unique Abundant Author blueprint (a blueprint that of course gets to evolve and shift over time). This will be your foundation for sharing. As you create your offer, you can start to weave elements of that into your content. But don't wait until you're clear on that! You know what your intention is. You know the work you're doing in the world. So you get to share and start creating new connections. Right now.

My Abundant Author Visibility Blueprint

My intention for sharing is to:

_____

_____

_____

The platforms I'm choosing to use are:

Core

_____

Secondary:

1) _____

2) _____

3) Optional _____

I'm choosing to share ……. times per week

Ideas for content:

Intimacy — stories/experiences I could share:

1)
2)
3)
4)
5)
6)
7)
8)
9)
10)

Inspiration — ideas/perspective shifts I could share:

1)
2)
3)
4)
5)
6)
7)
8)
9)
10)

Information — tips + guidance I could share

1)
2)
3)
4)
5)
6)
7)
8)
9)
10)

A final note, I've invited you to come up with 10 ideas for each energy. Of course, there will be more. And also, it's powerful to take the same idea and share it in different ways, from a slightly (or completely) different angle.

When it comes to visibility, you want to remember – repetition is your friend

People need to hear things often many times before it lands.

Don't shy away from talking about the same thing, over and over. Most likely no one will notice. And if they do, they'll thank you for it.

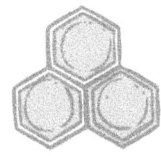

Compelling Offer Creation

Creating an Offer

Now that you've got clearer on how you want to be visible and connect with your people, let's dive into a vital aspect of the Abundant Author journey – creating an offer.

Not just any offer though! The one you get to create through this process is specifically designed to:

1) Amplify the message of your book

2) Provide a channel for greater financial abundance to flow to you

3) Enable you to be more deeply of service to your people.

I say 'one' but of course, you can (and may already) have more than one offer. For the purposes of your Abundant Author journey, we're going to focus on creating an offer that intentionally does all of the above. See it as a way of giving your book the opportunity to flourish into a more expansive expression of what it's here to be.

The offer you're about to create may represent the full journey you take your reader on or a smaller section of your book, like a chapter or a snippet.

It could also be a deepening of what you cover in your book or a next step.

What you're aiming for is an offering that when people read your book, they feel called to step into this next 'thing' with you.

They want to come closer.

They want to go deeper.

They want to connect more fully with the message you're sharing.

And you have at least one way they can do that.

So, what might that be?

Perhaps you have a one-to-one or group program that takes people on a similar journey to your book?

Maybe you offer a workshop or retreat that goes more deeply into one of the stages or chapters of your book?

Perhaps you organise an event or festival based on the message of your book?

The possibilities are limitless. And you get to choose whatever feels joyful, exciting, aligned and abundant to you, right now in this moment.

The invitation is to let this be easeful. There's no need to complicate things. How can you embrace the energy of simplicity?

Different Approaches

Before we dive into creating your Abundant Author offer, let's talk a little about the different approaches to offer creation.

Some people recommend having an offer ladder – a range of offers at different price points. I've tended to do this throughout my business. I've definitely found it helpful to have more entry-level, low-cost offers, alongside higher investment services. There are a number of reasons this feels good to me:

1) They can attract new people into my world.

2) It feels more inclusive to have offers that are accessible.

3) I personally enjoy the variety.

Side Note: Remember, you get to create what feels good for you. Yes, it's helpful to be clear about what your people need and want, but it's no good following that and creating something that feels misaligned.

So, one approach is to have an offer ladder and another is to have one signature offer. An example of this is Denise Duffield-Thomas' Money Bootcamp, which has been her main offer since 2013. Yes, it's evolved along the way. She's run it as a live program, a self-study course with a Facebook group and now it's a hybrid of that with the resources being self-study and her hosting monthly live coaching calls in her group. She often talks about the fact that with her marketing, all roads lead to Bootcamp.

Having one offer and directing everyone towards that makes sense. It keeps things simple. However, as the unbound, multifaceted being you are, it's possible you might find this restrictive.

I tried the 'one signature offer' approach in the early days of the Unbound Writing Mastermind. Yes, we also had publishing packages with The Unbound Press, but for a while there my only other offer was the Mastermind. It was only for a while though! I know that people in my audience are at different stages/places and it's important for me to reflect that in the offers I have. Creating some more bite-sized offers gave me the ability to be of service to more people.

As I write this, I'm feeling called back to more simplicity. As with everything on this unbound, creative journey, there's an ebb and flow. The most important thing is that whatever you offer, and how you offer it, feels abundant for you. This includes changing your mind when you feel called to, letting go of offers that no longer feel aligned and creating new ways for people to work with you.

I've been through so many evolutions in my author business, from the early days of Heal Your Inner Good Girl to where I am now, creating The Abundant Author Academy around the ideas coming through in this book.

I know you probably have ideas bubbling already. Exciting! I'll be guiding you through a process to get super-clear on what you want to create, how you want to offer it and (very importantly!) what price it will be.

But first, let me share a personal example with you.

Unbound YOU

When I was coming towards the end of writing my second book, *UNBOUND*, I felt called to create an offering based on the five principles of living unbound I share in the book. I didn't want to teach the principles as such – I wanted to create something that was experiential, where each woman would get the opportunity to live each principle more fully in her life.

So I put together an online group program called UNBOUND You. It ran for ten weeks and the invitation was to focus on one of the five principles every two weeks.

At the beginning of each two-week segment we would have a live call where I would share an activation. I'd talk a little about whichever principle we were focusing on followed by some kind of meditation or visualisation. Then there would be a play assignment, an invitation to experiment with exploring that fortnight's principle more fully. We'd get to talk about that some more on a group coaching call the following week.

I allowed myself to create something that felt good for me. UNBOUND You felt easeful and joyful to hold space for AND it was powerful and spacious for those stepping in. #winwin

I charged $497 as an early bird price and this eventually increased to $997. (I was living in the States at the time, so I was using US dollars.) I didn't overthink the price. I wanted to offer an early-bird discount as this was the first time I'd run UNBOUND You. I chose a figure that felt aligned for me.

I didn't have to create the whole thing in advance before I sold the program. I knew the content and inspiration was there in my book. And I also knew I could create a powerful meditation/activation for each of the principles as we went along.

I played to my strengths and desires.

And you get to do the same, magical one.

Over to You

So, let's heartstorm! I'm going to share some questions to help you tune into what wants to come through for you. Remember, the invitation is to keep this simple and joyful. You get to choose what feels most abundant for you.

You could create a macro-offer that reflects the full journey you take your readers on in your book, or you might prefer a micro-offer where you focus on one element of your book.

Take some time to reflect on these questions:

What's the transformation you feel most passionate about holding space for right now?

What element of your book feels most inspiring to you when it comes to creating an offer?

What kind of offer would your book most like to be the foundation for?

How would you most like to work with people:

One-to-one or small or large groups?

Online or in-person?

Shorter or longer term?

Deep dive or an overview?

Would you prefer your offer to be always open or only open for a set period of time?

If you have existing offers, then ask:

Could I elevate/amplify an existing offer, providing a more immersive experience for clients who are happy to invest more to access a bigger or quicker transformation? (Perhaps including more one-to-one, bespoke support.)

Could I take one element of an existing offer and adapt it into a smaller, more entry-level service/product for those who want to dip their toe and take the first step with me?

Is there an existing offer that feels like it could be my signature Abundant Author offering?

Don't worry if not all of the details land straight away. This kind of reflective process can take a few days (or weeks). Clarity can drop in at random times. Online business specialist Elizabeth Goddard talks about the 'Shower Gods' who bless her with the most brilliant ideas when she's in the shower. For me it often happens when I'm out for a walk.

By taking time to ponder the above questions, you're opening a door to whatever offer wants to come through for you at this time. Allow everything to percolate and bubble away in the background as you move through the rest of this section.

What to call it?

Once you have even a glimpse of an idea of what your offer might be, start feeling into the name. Again, don't overthink this. You might use a similar name to your book. I've used Unbound in one way or another MANY times!

Unbound YOU

Unbound Writing Mastermind

Unbound Book Incubator

The Unbound Writer's Club membership

I'm sure there are more I'm forgetting! The truth is people won't pay much attention to the name you choose. Yes it's important to pick a name that expresses what your offer actually is, but I can guarantee that people will often call it something completely different to the name you've chosen.

So, keep it simple. And know you can change the name later as your offer evolves.

Okay, so now you have at least some of the details of the offer, let's move onto what can be a tricky part of the process for many soul-led entrepreneurs – how much to charge?

Potent Pricing

Let me ask you a question, magical one. Can you remember the first time you asked for money in exchange for the work you do?

I can. And it was pretty darn uncomfortable. I was a newly qualified hypnotherapist and although I'd done some practice sessions with friends, this was the first time working with somebody who was actually going to pay me.

I'd decided on my fee, £40 per hour. I settled on this amount after looking at what other hypnotherapists were charging in my area and then choosing a slightly lower rate than most of them. (Because how could I possibly charge as much as someone who was more experienced than me?) But, even though I'd chosen to charge a purposely low fee, I couldn't quite believe that someone was choosing to sit in a room with me for an hour and then give me £40 for the privilege. (I seem to have completely forgotten the fact that I'd trained long and hard to be able to share the benefits that hypnotherapy could provide to my client.)

When it came to the end of the session, I dreaded asking for the money. In fact, I waited until the client mentioned paying. And as she handed me the £40, I sheepishly accepted it. This was back in 2010 when I started my business. And as you can tell, I didn't particularly value the service I was offering at the time. The way I saw it, my clients were paying for my time. One hour = £40 (or £200 for six sessions if you paid in advance). I didn't appreciate that clients pay for an outcome, not time, and my prices needed to reflect that.

I had a WHOLE load of limiting beliefs and old unhelpful stories running about money, that made it virtually impossible to set prices that would enable me to have a sustainable business. The truth is it's no good looking OUTSIDE to get the answers when it comes to pricing. You need to look within.

Over the years since then, I've realised that pricing isn't just a logical, financial decision. And it's certainly not a case of researching other businesses who offer the same as you and then pitching your prices somewhere in the middle. (Or posting in a Facebook group asking how much other people think you should charge for a particular product or service.) Pricing is often an energetic decision – it's influenced by the way you feel about yourself and what you have to offer. It depends on the underlying beliefs you have about money and success.

And that's good news. Because you get to create the energetic shift that allows you to choose prices that feel truly abundant, whilst at the same time attracting more of your people.

The truth is when you're undercharging and over-giving, you're not serving yourself or your clients. That's why I'm dedicating this whole section to pricing. After working with many spiritual authors and entrepreneurs over the past 10 years, I've realised that there are some essential questions that will enable you to set aligned, sustainable prices which allow you to feel well-rewarded.

Now, I'm going to share them with you, so you can land on the initial price for your Abundant Author offer. I say 'initial price' because like everything we're creating in this process, it gets to evolve and shift. Reminding yourself of that will liberate you from the 'must get this right!' trap that many of us fall into.

Please know, you can't get this wrong. I invite you to have fun with the questions I'm guiding you through here. Adopt an attitude of playful exploration as you go through them. The truth is YOU are the expert in your business. No one can tell you what you should or shouldn't do. So, imagine you have a clear, blank page in front of you. This is your chance to let go of anything you may have been told, any 'helpful' advice you've been given by friends or family, or anything you've felt you 'should' be doing.

By asking yourself these questions, you get to access your own inner knowing and unlock the natural abundance that's already there within you. (Because it REALLY is there.)

Question One: How much do you WANT to earn?

This may seem like an obvious question. But are you truly clear on how much money you want to create in your Abundant Author business?

When I used to ask clients this question, many of them initially came up with a figure based on how much they need to earn – just enough to cover their expenses, plus a little bit more.

Side Note: Whenever you use the word 'need' it's possible you're coming from a place of fear and lack. When you switch to thinking about what you 'want', you move into an energy of excitement and expansion. This makes it much easier to attract what you desire into your Abundant Author business.

So, let me ask you – Is 'just enough' really enough for you? I don't think so! You deserve to be abundantly rewarded for the work you do. That's the whole point of this book. And if you don't truly believe that, stick with me, we're going to get to your beliefs soon.

SO, let's go again – how much do you want to earn, magical one?

Start playing with some figures – monthly and annual amounts. Write some numbers down, say them out loud, notice what figures come to mind. As you experiment with different incomes, notice how you feel about each one. If a number feels constrictive or leaves you feeling flat and deflated, move on and up. Your aim is to choose a number that feels expansive, exciting, stretchy enough to feel compelling, inspiring enough to make you want to take action.

But of course, you'll want to work through the rest of the questions before you get going – clarity is the KEY.

How much do you want to earn?

Question Two: What are ALL the ways your offer benefits your people?

I'm sure the main benefit of the offer you're feeling called to create is clear to you, but when you're thinking about pricing, I want you to look deeper than the topline benefit. Give yourself at least 10 minutes on this question and heartstorm all the ways a client benefits from investing in this offer.

Really go to town and think about all the areas of their life that could be impacted. For example, the main benefit of working with me in The Abundant Author Academy is that someone gets to create a compelling, soul-aligned offer around their writing giving them an additional income stream. But alongside that they also:

- Start to express more of their magic in the world
- Get clearer on their Abundant Author business model, leading to more focus and more time to do the things they love
- Sell more copies of their book
- Become more comfortable with money (and receiving larger amounts of it)
- Gain greater confidence in who they are and what they're here to do
- Have a bigger impact with their work
- Feel comfortable being more visible in their business
- Attract more soul-aligned clients
- Fall more deeply in love with the work they're here to do.

Etc, etc, etc! You can see how once you get on a roll, this list can be endless and you get a really clear sense of the value you have to offer to your people.

To help with this, look back at any feedback and testimonials you've received from previous clients. Once you've tuned into all the ways your offer benefits a client, you can begin to get a sense of a price that reflects this (and very often, it will be higher than you initially thought).

What are ALL the ways your offer benefits people?

Question 3: What are your beliefs around money and pricing?

This is a biggie and let's face it, this could be a whole book of its own.

The beliefs you have help to shape your reality. So, let's say you're a relationship coach and you want to charge £2,000 for a VIP Day, but you have a belief running that says 'Who am I kidding? No one will be willing to pay that much.' Guess what? That's likely to be reflected back at you. You'll either find it hard to attract clients in the first place, or any prospective clients you do speak to won't be willing to invest at that level.

Other common beliefs I've heard around pricing are:

'No one will pay that much in the area where I live.'

'People won't pay that much for what I have to offer.'

'This comes so naturally to me, I can't charge much for it.'

'It would have to be really hard work to make that much money.'

'I'm not worth that much.'

The fact is there's a shed-load of second-guessing going on around pricing. Many soul-led entrepreneurs make HUGE assumptions about what their potential clients would be willing to pay. And there's a prevalent belief that you have to suffer, struggle and work really damn hard to make good money.

Now, I'm not bypassing the fact that we live in a world where there are a number of oppressive systems at play – hello, Patriarchy, capitalism, white supremacy. And there's also fierce inequality. But we still get to play our part in changing the game.

What if we could see some of the statements I've shared above as stories we tell ourselves?

I mean, we're writers aren't we? So how about we write some new stories?

The idea that you can't charge much for something that comes naturally to you? Er, nah! The fact the magic you make feels easy for you means that when you do it, you're in flow. Your people, who are struggling in the area where you're flowing, need your help and are willing to pay for it.

The idea that people won't be willing to pay much in your geographical location or area of expertise? Poppycock! There are clients at all levels of investment – low, medium and high (which is all relative of course). You can choose which you want to work with and set your pricing accordingly.

I'm sure you've done a load of work around your money mindset in the past and are familiar with your 'stuff', but as you think about putting your Abundant Author offer out there, I invite you to check out your beliefs around pricing. Notice the stories you're telling yourself right now. And if you feel they're restricting your sense of what's possible, resolve to rewrite them.

Hint: Just bringing these old, limiting stories into your awareness is a powerful step towards changing them. As you work through the other questions in this section, just set your intention to notice any doubts or fears that bubble to the surface and write them down. Rather than beating yourself up for feeling that way, be grateful that another limiting belief or old story has come into your awareness. This is ALWAYS the first step to change.

What beliefs are bubbling up for me right now around money and pricing?

Question 4: How many of your offer will you need to sell in order to reach your income goal?

Okay, so now you've tuned into what you want, the value of what you have to offer and your beliefs, it's time to do a simple calculation. This is going to help you to get really clear on your prices. From the exploration you've done already, decide on an initial investment for your offer. (You know what I'm going to say here, right? DON'T overthink it!)

Once you have that, divide your monthly income goal by the price of your offer to calculate the amount you'd need to sell each month.

How many of your offer will you need to sell in order to reach your income goal?

Now you have this number, it's time to move on to the final question, which is...

Question 5: How does this FEEL?

Once you know how much you'd need to sell in order to reach your monthly income goal, ask yourself, 'How does this feel?'

Does it feel sustainable or exhausting?

Does it feel achievable or impossible?

Does it feel expansive or constricting?

Only you can answer these questions.

Hint: If you're finding it difficult to get clear on how you feel about this, notice how your body feels as you think about it. Your body will ALWAYS give you the answer, so notice if you feel tense or relaxed, heavy or light, tired or energised. By getting out of your head and into your body, you access a source of deep inner wisdom.

If you find the investment you've initially chosen makes you feel like you're going to have to run yourself ragged to achieve the income you desire, then resistance and self-sabotage are likely to kick in (and you'll find it difficult to attract clients). In contrast, if your pricing means that you can serve your clients at the level you want to, whilst still meeting your needs, then business will flow much more easily.

How does this feel?

Now that you've moved through the rest of the questions, this is the point where you can begin to adjust your pricing to get it in that sweet, oh-so-abundant spot.

Hint: When your pricing is in that sweet spot, you'll attract more of your soul-aligned people. I suggest working through these questions at least annually, as your energetic income level shifts and grows, and also whenever you launch a new product or service.

Please know, pricing is always going to be a work in progress. The invitation is to land on an initial price now, knowing you can change it in the future. There's no 'right' answer, so allow yourself to choose a price that feels good and trust that. As with everything on this Abundant Author journey, you get to course-correct as you go.

Enticing Invitations

Okay, magical soul, once you know what your offer is going to be and have decided on an initial price, it's time to create an invitation.

You might call this a sales page. And that can conjure up thoughts of fancy design and techy issues. But have no fear. It doesn't have to be complicated.

You can keep this as simple as you like. In case you hadn't realised, the idea on your Abundant Author journey is to do everything in a way that makes it as ease-ful as possible for you to move forward and be the channel of abundance you're here to be.

So, yes, you could create a full-blown sales page on your website if that feels good.

Or you could:

Write a bunch of emails and/or social media posts inviting your people into your offer.

Create a Google Doc with the details and share that with anyone who's interested.

Send personal messages or voice notes to those you think might be interested in what you're creating.

We're going to be talking more about launching in the next section. (Don't freak out – we're not going to be all hustle-y about it. Laid-back launching is the vibe.)

For now, I want you to write a simple invitation to your people, outlining the details of your offer, who it's for, what challenges it can help with and what kind of outcomes it can help to create.

When I'm writing an invitation for a new offer, I like to imagine I'm writing a letter to the person I'd most love to work with. It can be tempting to slip into 'information mode' and lose the excitement you felt when you were tuning into the idea for your offering. We don't want that.

Let your words run free, magical one. And allow abundance to stream through each one.

A Final Word on Offers

Whatever you create in your business, you get to check in with the energy of it. Just like I recommend you do with your book(s), you can connect with the different elements of your biz – whether that's offerings, platforms, systems, teams.

What I've found is that this can cut through any uncertainty and complication, getting straight to the heart of the various elements of your business.

For example, as I launched the new Birth Your Transformational Book program, I was curious about how it might be different to the Unbound Writing Mastermind I'd run previously. Some of the content would be the same. I was still hosting group writing sessions and coaching calls. Would it really feel that different?

The answer was 'Yes!' As I tuned into BYTB on the first day it opened, there was a new clarity streaming through the program that I hadn't connected with before. It was a quality I know I'd been called to bring through more of. And by making changes in my business, letting go of previous offerings, like the UWM, and creating new ones, like BYTB, this new energy had somewhere to land.

And this is important to acknowledge. Because sometimes when we're called to make changes, it might not make logical sense.

I'd been running the UWM for 5+ years.

The members loved it.

It was a powerful and magical space.

And people knew about it as my signature, core offering.

So, why on earth would I choose to close it and create something new?

I couldn't quite put it into words.

Because it was more of a feeling.

Fortunately, the magical beings in the Unbound Writing community get it. When I shared my decision with them, they completely understood and were excited to be part of the new spaces I was being called to create.

But it's only when the new spaces opened that I could REALLY connect with the specific energy that was wanting to come through them.

The sparkling clarity of BYTB blew me away. It was palpable. And I'm so glad I trusted the initial impulse to create this new offering.

Now you get to do the same.

Laid-Back Launching

Launching

There's a lot of talk around launching in the entrepreneurial space. And of course, in the publishing space.

Whether you're launching a book, a product or some other kind of offering, it can feel like a lot of effort. The very word 'launch' suggests getting something up off the ground and into the air. It can feel like an intense rush of energy is needed/required. And that might feel overwhelming for a magical being like you.

Maybe you've seen the big names doing huge, elaborate launches with all the bells and whistles?

Webinars.

Three-part video series.

Maybe a challenge?

Endless emails, podcast appearances, media mentions and affiliates.

Do you really have to launch that way?

Of course not.

If the bells and whistles approach feels good to you, fill your bountiful boots.

But if the very idea of it brings on a feeling of dread, you get to do this your own sweet way.

In reality, a launch is simply a window of time when you're promoting (sharing) a particular offer. That period of time could be 24 hours, a week, a month or longer. The idea is to create energy around what you're offering, let people know about it and invite them to buy.

The way you do that is up to you and the possibilities are endless.

You could focus on sending a series of emails.

You might share on social media.

Video or lives might be your jam.

Or maybe you go back to basics and connect with people one-to-one.

And of course, you could combine two or more different approaches.

I personally like the following recipe for launching:

Start with a medley of social media posts and emails.

Add one 3-5 day online community experience – I'm going to be sharing more about this shortly.

Sprinkle over another handful of emails and social media posts at the end.

I like this approach because community is a core value for both me and The Unbound Press. I do work with a handful of one-to-one clients, but most of my offerings are group-based. So having some kind of community experience – a challenge or a coaching series – gives my people a taste of how I hold space.

If you can mirror your particular offering as you're launching, it makes it easier for people to step in. So, if you're focusing on one-to-one work, you might want to offer exploratory calls or the opportunity to connect with you in the DMs.

What I've realised over years of launching in various ways is that it's important not to get attached to any particular outcome. Yes, it can be powerful to have a goal in mind, but sometimes/often the results of a launch can show up in unexpected ways.

I've learned this through personal experience; the times when I've done a launch and not attracted the number of people I'd hoped into a program, but perhaps someone decided to sign up as a one-to-one client. Or the connections I've made with existing and new people during the launch have led to them working with me a few months (or even years) down the line.

My aim now is always to focus on relationships during any launch. You never know where they may lead. Remember how we reframed visibility as connection earlier on? Well, it's the same with launching. Rather than placing your focus on trying to get more people to buy your stuff, what if you could see launching as an opportunity to connect with more people (and connect more deeply with those who are already in your world)?

To me, that feels incredibly liberating.

It takes the pressure off.

And yes, of course, the intention is for you to sell your Abundant Author offer through the launch process. But the outcome gets to be so much more than that.

How does your offer want to be launched?

So, now it's time for you to tune into how you want to launch your offer. (Or rather, how your offer wants to be launched.)

As I mentioned in the previous section, it's most powerful if the way you launch reflects your offer in some way.

So, if you're going to be working with people one-to-one, you might want to share about the offer – perhaps via email, social media, a Masterclass or webinar – with the intention of inviting people into a discovery call with you.

If it's a group journey you're going to be taking people on, then it's helpful to give your audience a taste of that by creating some kind of community experience. This is one of my fave ways to launch an offering. And even if your intention is to work with people one-to-one, it can be a powerful way to give them a flavour of how you hold space.

I'm going to guide you through the process of creating a community experience now, so you can feel the potential and start to get excited around how you might incorporate this in your own launch. Because connection is such a big part of the Abundant Author process, launching in community can feel especially aligned.

This may be what you choose to do. It may not be. You may choose to play with elements of what I share here. You may choose to go your own unique way. But I wanted to give you an overview of creating this kind of event for your community so you can decide for yourself.

Creating a Community Experience as Part of Your Launch

A community experience can be any kind of event where you're inviting people to come together. It could absolutely be an in-person event that you choose to host. However, to keep things simple here I'm focusing on an online event where you take your people on some kind of a journey.

I'm sure you've probably been part of something similar in the past. Maybe you've taken part in a challenge or online coaching series? You might even have taken part in our annual Unbound Book-Writing Challenge. As you move through this section, remember how it felt to be part of someone else's community experience. What felt good? What might you do differently? Remember, you get to do this YOUR way (and, as ever, you can't get it wrong!).

Intention + Focus

When you decide to run an event like this, the first thing is to get clear on your overall intention. Take some time to journal on the questions:

How do you want to feel as you host your community experience?

How do you want your people to feel?

What's the next step you want to invite people into? Are you planning to invite them directly into your Abundant Author offer, or do you want to have a one-to-one conversation with them first? Maybe there's some kind of application process to work with you in the offer you've created? If that's the case, the next step would be for them to complete that.

Once you're clear on your intention, you get to tune into the focus for your community experience:

What do you want to teach/hold space for?

What's the journey you're taking your participants on?

Is there a process you'll take them through?

How might this lead into your offer?

You've heard me say this before in these pages, but I recommend you keep things simple here. As the magical, unbound being you are, you probably want to give your people the most powerful experience. You might imagine that to do this you need to pull out all the stops, sharing everything you possibly can around the topic you've chosen.

But no. This is the way to overwhelm. The idea here is to give people a taste of working with you, to help them have a perspective shift, to see what's possible – not to load them up with information.

The key word here is: *experience.* You want to leave space for your people to have an experience. A powerful one. And you can do that by sharing some juicy morsels throughout your event.

Honestly, I've learned this the hard way. When I ran my first community experiences, I threw so much into it that people ended up feeling super-full. There was no space for them to want to move forward. And many of the participants dropped off through the five days of the event as it felt too much for them.

So, I've learned to keep it (relatively!) simple. I certainly don't withhold information or insight. As people ask questions or share challenges, I respond to them. However, I also make it clear that to go deeper and get ongoing support, I recommend stepping into whatever offer I'm sharing.

Logistics

So, you've set your intention and decided on the focus for your community experience. Now you get to land on the logistics.

How long?

The first thing to decide is how long your event will be. It could absolutely be a one-off session, like a workshop or Masterclass, but in my experience taking people on a journey over a period of days is more powerful. The reason for this comes back to connection. When you run a one-off session, yes, the attendees get to connect with you, but they don't have much opportunity to connect with each other. Now if you're inviting people into a one-to-one offer, that's not an issue. However, if you're asking them to join some kind of group journey, then it's helpful for them to have an idea of what it's like to be in one of your communities, to get to know others and how you hold space for a group.

I used to run challenges over five days, but have now landed on three. It can be hard for people to stay in momentum for five days. Three feels much more manageable for them, and often for you as the host.

Where?

Now you get to decide where to host your event. You ideally want a platform where people get to connect with both you AND each other.

There are plenty of options for this (and by the time you read this, there will probably be a ton more!). I recommend choosing somewhere you're familiar with. So, if you use Zoom to run group calls, you can run sessions on there. But I'd also recommend having a space where people can connect in-between any live sessions. This could be something like a pop-up Facebook group, a Telegram channel or WhatsApp group – I won't list out all the options as, like I've just alluded to, they're changing all the time. The key is to choose a way that feels aligned for you, and hopefully for your people.

I've personally tended to use Facebook groups for my community experiences. They're not ideal and I realise not everybody is on Facebook, but most of my people are and it's somewhere they naturally hang out. That makes it easy for them to join the pop-up group and engage.

Paid/Unpaid?

Traditionally most community experiences have been free, particularly when they're part of a launch, but this is starting to shift. There's been a rise in the number of paid-for online events, like challenges, bootcamps and workshops.

The idea in having a fee for an event like this is that although you'll have fewer people joining, the ones who do are more committed. So, they're more likely to take the next step with you afterwards.

I've gone both ways. When I ran my first community experiences, they were free to join. Then I started to offer the annual Unbound Writing Challenge on a pay-what-you-choose basis with a suggested donation. And as I write this, most recently I've switched back to free. The reason for that is my intention – in this season I'm wanting to connect with a wider audience. I want to reach people who are completely new to the world of Unbound, so I want to make it as easy as possible for them to step in.

In previous seasons my intention has been to connect more deeply with people who were most likely already aware of the Unbound community in some way, so I was happy to charge a fee.

Again, there's no right (or wrong) answer here. Go with what feels good for you and know you can always experiment with doing it differently next time.

Other Considerations

Once you've landed on how long, where and free or paid, there are a few other things to consider.

Do you want people to sign up to your email list in order to join your community experience?

Ideally, I'd recommend yes, as you want to have a way of staying in touch with them even if they don't join your offer. But in the past I've run online events where I've simply invited people to join a Facebook group to be part of it. These have usually been times when I wanted to keep it super-simple, for me and those joining.

Do you want to run any sessions live or pre-record them?

As part of your experience, it's likely you'll want to show up for your people with some kind of teaching or training, so you get to decide whether to do that live or to pre-record. Again this comes down to what feels most comfortable and aligned to you.

For me, I've pretty much always decided to run live sessions as I prefer to have interaction and the potential for deeper connection. As a Manifesting Generator in human design, I thrive on having something or someone to respond to, so being in the moment with my people works best. For you, it might be different, so trust that.

Invitation

Now you know what your event will be and how you're going to run it, you want to think about how to invite people to be part of it.

You can do this in different ways. Maybe you'll create a sign-up page on your website? Perhaps you share a social media post (or more powerfully, posts!) with the details? Send an email or create a Google Doc. Of course, you could do ALL of these

The key is to share the details in a simple way, letting people know why they want to join, what you'll support them with, when and where your event is happening and how to be part of it.

I recommend sharing for two weeks before your community experience. If you try and invite people much before that, they'll probably put off signing up until nearer the time. Most will join at the last minute, so don't be disheartened if the flow is slow to start off with. Keep sharing right up until your event starts and for the first day as well. That's often when the energy is most magnetic, because you're beginning to work your magic!

A question that can trip up many aspiring, abundant authors is, *How do I find people who will want to be part of my community experience?*

If you have a community already – an email list, peeps on social media, clients, past and present – amazing! You get to share the invitation far and wide with them.

But if you haven't got a community (or a teeny tiny one), then there are a couple of things I want you to know:

1) Firstly, never underestimate the power of a tiny community! Even if you have a handful of people, absolutely invite them to join you. The magic has to begin somewhere and it gets to start with those you're already in connection with.

2) Are there other people who can help you share your event? Do you have friends, colleagues, clients, acquaintances and mentors who could share the word for you? All too often we shy away from asking people for help

when in reality they would LOVE to support us. Being open to receive is a key part of the Abundant Author journey, so you can start by asking for what you want here.

3) As people join your community experience, ask them to share the invitation with others who might be interested. I've often created a simple graphic with the details of my event and asked those who've already signed up to share it with their people. But if you don't feel called or able to do that, just ask them to share the invitation – whether that's a webpage, a social media post or something else.

The magic gets to ripple out! Your first event may be small and intimate, but over time you'll reach more people.

Host it!

Okay, so you've done all the prep, you've invited your people and now you get to do your thing – hosting your event.

Here are some things to bear in mind as you do:

Energy

Remember when you set an intention about how you want to feel during your community experience? How can you allow that to happen?

Clear Space

In the past I've made the mistake of thinking I could rock up and do a daily Facebook live for my challenge, whilst still maintaining my regular schedule. And the thing is I CAN do this, but I'm not at my best when I approach it like this.

Your community experience is important. You're holding space for people to have a transformation. You're inviting people to come closer and hopefully take the next step with you. You're sharing more of your magic with the world.

So you want to honour that.

I recommend clearing your schedule as much as possible for the time you're running your event. That way you get to be fully in it.

Support

What kind of support might you need as you run your community experience?

This could be something like asking your partner to cook dinner or look after the kids more than usual. Or it could be having an assistant helping you to manage the Facebook group.

Maybe you book an extra session with your energy healer or coach?

Perhaps you're more intentional about getting out for a daily walk or spending time in meditation?

Calling in support from your team, seen and unseen, is key here.

Notice What's Happening & Capture Feedback

This is also key. It can be easy to get swept up in holding space for your people and focusing on the offer you're launching, and forget to allow yourself to really BE in the experience.

There's the potential for so much richness in these community events, regardless of the outcome. Notice what's bubbling up for people as they go on the journey with you. Questions, challenges and insights that arise can be a powerful source of future content.

As people are giving feedback, sharing successes and breakthroughs, keep a record of this in some way. I recommend taking screenshots that you can store for yourself and also ask the person who commented whether they'd be happy for you to share in your marketing and promotion.

Enjoy It!

Following on from the last point, remember to enjoy your community experience. The whole idea of the Abundant Author process is that it gets to spark abundance in countless different ways. If you're not enjoying the journey, what's the point?

I'm not saying there won't be challenges along the way and you may well experience expansion sensations as you run your event, but you also get to enjoy the ride.

What happens next?

Okay, so as you come to the end of your community experience, it's important to remember what's next. As you've been running your event as a way to launch your Abundant Author offer, you want to invite people to take the next step with you.

Now, the conventional way of doing this was to wait until the last day and then do a pitch. But this can feel icky for many magical peeps (like you). The truth is there very well could be people who are ready and wanting to work with you from the moment they step into your community experience. And certainly participants will start to ponder on the possibility as they journey with you. So I tend to talk about whatever it is I'm offering throughout my event, weaving in details whenever it feels relevant and letting my people know that I'll be inviting them to join me as a next step.

So, talk about your offer during the event and also send emails with the details when it comes to an end.

But that's not all. Your community experience is just the beginning (and I've definitely forgotten this in the past). Follow-up is vital. I've often expected people to sign-up straight away when I make the invitation and in my experience that's often not the case.

People will sometimes want to have a one-to-one connection with you before stepping into your offer. They may have questions or fears about joining. It's important to give them a way of contacting you – this could be a call, but it could just as easily be a voice note or text message in the DMs.

If someone's been particularly engaged in your event or you feel that a person might be a great fit for your offer, reach out personally and let them know. Now, I'm not talking sleazy, pushy, awkward messages – that's not the Abundant Author vibe and I know it's not yours either. Remember this is all about connection. So you get to connect with anyone who feels especially aligned and give them the opportunity to ask you anything that might be bubbling.

An example. There's a person who always showed up for your live sessions during the event, they engaged every day and asked questions, plus they were always supportive of other group members. You could drop them a message thanking them for being such an engaged member of the experience and asking them if they know what their next step might be?

They may or may not be thinking about joining your offer, but that personal connection helps to deepen your relationship.

We talked about creating space when you're running your event. I also encourage you to leave space afterwards, so you can follow up, be available to answer questions and connect with people one-to-one.

Reflect & Review

The final step? Once you've run your event, made your invitation and followed up with your participants, take some time to reflect on the experience and harvest any learnings around what you might do differently next time.

The first time you run something like this can feel clunky. It may well not flow the way you expect. And that's okay. As with everything on your Abundant Author journey, it gets to evolve.

Ask yourself these questions:

What went well with my community experience?

What did I enjoy about it?

What did the participants find most powerful?

What felt challenging?

What would I do differently next time?

What were the outcomes:

   1) In terms of launching my offer?

   2) Other, perhaps unexpected, outcomes?

Over to You

So, magical one, that's given you a flavour of how you might incorporate some kind of community experience into your launch. I know it can feel like a lot of moving parts, but honestly the way I've learned is to make a decision and run one.

As you navigate your Abundant Author journey, this is a key skill – that willingness to experiment, try things out, see what works (and what doesn't). And the thing is, when you allow yourself to do this, you really can't fail. Because each time you have a go at something new, you'll learn so much.

Remember, everything is an opportunity for deeper connection.

With yourself.

With your people.

With what you're called to create.

With the Abundant Author you are.

I've given you a lot of inspiration here about how you could create a community event as the centre of your launch. Now you get to feel into what approach would be most aligned for you (and your offer).

The best way to do that?

I'm sure as you were reading through the last section, you had a felt sense of what you'd like to do, what felt exciting, expansive and abundant. You also get to ask your offer.

Yep, your offer. Because, of course, it has an energy, an essence, a spirit of its own. And it will have its own ideas about how it wants to be launched into the world.

So, take some time now to connect with the essence of your offer.

Get quiet, take some deep breaths and invite it to connect with you.

Maybe you experience your Abundant Author offer visually, as a colour or image?

Perhaps you have a felt sense of its energy?

You might hear it.

As ever, know that however it comes into your presence is perfect. Even if you don't have a clear sense of it at all, you get to receive answers to the questions you're about to ask.

As you connect, ask your offer:

How would you like me to share you?

How can I help you reach the people you're here for?

What's the most abundant way for me to invite people into you?

Feel free to ask any other questions you have. If you're not sure about particular details of your launch, consult with your offer. Know that it's your co-creative partner and will be delighted to help. If the answers don't drop in immediately, they can arrive in the hours and days after you've connected.

Take some time to write your insights and ideas here:

Collaboration & Community

Deepening your Impact

Okay, magical one, now that you've started to embody the Abundant Author you are more fully by experimenting with vibrant visibility, compelling offer creation and laid-back launching, we get to explore the final piece of the puzzle – deepening your impact through collaboration and creating community.

This has been the magic sauce in my own business. The connections I've made and the opportunities they've led to, often unexpectedly, have been a key in bringing me to where I am now – the founder of a publishing company with a community of soul-led, Unbound writers. If it hadn't been for the energy of collaboration, The Unbound Press would never have been a thing. The idea came through my connection with someone else – the brilliant Sean Patrick of The Good House Publishing. As soon as he mentioned the idea, I KNEW in my bones this was what I was meant to do. But would I have realised this without his initial input? I'm really not sure.

This is just one example of hundreds I've experienced over the years I've been in business. The truth is everything is co-created. Everything.

We may think an idea – whether it's for a book, an offer, a social media post – has come purely through us, but that's impossible. We are all connected. We are continually being inspired and activated by others. And everything comes from this potent soup of our inter-connectedness.

I'm a big believer that we can't help but end up where we're meant to be, doing what we're meant to do and connecting with the people we're meant to. Being open to collaboration and community is a way to super-charge and often speed up this process.

We've already touched on the magic of community when talking about launching. In this section, we'll look at how you can create a space or platform for your people and how to invite more of the energy of collaboration into your business.

Reflecting on Collaboration

Before we dive in, let me ask you a couple of questions:

What's been your previous experience of collaboration?

Can you think of at least one example of something you've co-created in your business with another person (or people)?

How did the opportunity come about?

What did you enjoy about it?

What didn't feel so good?

How do you feel about entering into another collaboration?

Take some time to reflect on these questions and notice what bubbles up. Do you feel excited about the possibilities or is there any lingering resentment or resistance around collaborations you've experienced in the past?

If you're aware of any contraction, know that this time you get to do things differently. You get to enter into this process with more intention. Everything you've learned so far on your Abundant Author journey will serve you well here.

When I first started venturing into the online space with my business, there was a lot of talk of Joint Ventures. Everyone seemed to be teaming up – inviting their audience to attend a friend's webinar, being a guest expert in someone else's course, offering a call as a bonus when you signed up to someone's program. On the surface it all looked aligned and collaborative. But often underneath, it was purely transactional.

I remember being on a call with a time management expert, which had been included as a bonus when I signed up to work with my first business coach. I very soon realised the point of this call wasn't to help me with my time management. No, it was a discovery call in disguise. Her aim was to sell me into one of her programs. It felt deeply uncomfortable to be put in this position. I'd just invested a substantial amount in the first group coaching program I'd ever been part of and wasn't at all ready to think about investing with anyone else. And the thing is, this was just one of a series of 'bonus' calls I'd been offered when I joined. This coach had teamed up with many of her ex-clients to try and funnel new people towards their work whilst presenting the opportunity to connect with them as a 'bonus'.

This was the way things were done 'back then'. And I'm sure it's still going on. But this is NOT true collaboration. And it's definitely not the vibe we're going for here.

If you've had ick experiences of collaboration in the past, let me remind you again – we get to do things differently.

Being Open

There will be times when you seek out opportunities for collaboration, maybe when you want to reach a new audience or you're putting together some kind of project and you're looking for others to be involved. We'll absolutely talk about that in a while, but just as powerful are those times when unexpected possibilities flow your way, when connections lead to all sorts of unplanned magic.

I've experienced many of these in the past. Pretty much every single member of The Unbound Press team are people I connected with one way or another LONG before I started the company. Some I've worked with as a client, some have been clients of mine and some have been co-creative partners in other ways.

Our marketing and podcast whiz, Jo Gifford and I were initially connected via a group program we were both part of. I went on to be a client in one of her courses (which was brilliant!) and this deepened our connection. She then saw I'd started The Unbound Press and reached out to publish a book with us and that led to her coming onboard as a team member.

One of our designers, Leah Kent, and I have been connected since she signed up for a free call with me back in 2015 (I think!). We immediately resonated with each other, so we kept in touch and co-created a class around intuition a couple of years afterwards. After that I did one of her courses in Tarot and she became a founding member of The Unbound Writing Mastermind, before joining The Unbound Press team.

You get a sense of that glorious soup of interconnectedness I talked about earlier. There's no way any of us could have strategically planned out what would come from our connections. The energy has ebbed and flowed between us. It's all felt beautifully organic. Abundance in action.

So, my invitation to you is to be open. And to know, the more you connect, the more people you allow yourself to be in connection with and the deeper those connections, the more magic gets sparked.

I bet it's already happening in your life. Take some time to reflect on the people you've connected with in your business. What examples can you think of where a connection has led to co-creation and opportunity?

But what if I'm an introvert?

As you're reading this section, you might be thinking, 'But Nicola, I'm an introvert. I suck at meeting new people. It drains me.'

I hear you. Me too! I have strong introvert tendencies and I've always felt clumsy when it comes to putting myself 'out there'. Even now if I'm in a group where I don't know anyone, I'll be the gal hiding out on the edges. There have been (many) times when I've been at events where I've seen someone I know online and I've been scared to go over and say 'hello'.

Many of us have the lone wolf thing going on. We've picked up the message that we should be able to do 'it' on our own and/or we've felt burned by our connection with others in the past. So, we've put our blinkers on and made the decision to walk this path alone.

Writing a book can be a solitary process. That's at least part of the reason why a lot of us are attracted to it in the first place! It's something we get to do ourselves with no input from others. What a relief!

But I recommend going against the grain when it comes to this. A big part of the Unbound Writing approach I teach is to create community around your writing. That way it gets to be a dynamic, interactive process. The same goes for the Abundant Author journey.

The good news? You can do this in an introvert-friendly way.

Rather than focusing on one-to-many connections, you get to send tendrils out to one aligned soul at a time. You get to go gently.

Maybe that looks like starting a conversation with someone you resonate with online (and that can be as simple as leaving a thoughtful comment on one of their posts).

Perhaps you reach out to that woman in the Mastermind you're part of who feels like a kindred soul and suggest a virtual coffee date? (I bet she'd be delighted!)

Or you might offer the chance to have one-to-one connection calls with those who are already on your email list or in your world in some way?

It's all about deepening.

This is how you put yourself in the way of magic. And open to abundance.

Abundant Author Assignment: Make it your mission to connect more deeply with one new person each week. Let go of any expectations about where it might lead. Simply have the intention to create connection. Before you know it, you'll have a web of magical new beings in your world.

Taking the Lead – Creating Your Own Collaborative Opportunities

Okay, so up until now we've been talking about harnessing the power of organic connections and following the flow. If you're ready (or at least willing) to step in more fully, I invite you to think about creating your own collaborative opportunity.

What does this look like? Well, what I mean is putting together some kind of event (online or in-person) and inviting others to be part of it. This could be a summit, an interview series, a bundle, a community project, a festival or event.

Hosting your own event means you benefit in a number of ways:

- You get to choose the theme of the event.
- You get to choose who's part of it (and create a deeper connection with each person involved).
- You get to grow your email list, as generally each person who signs up to be part of an event will provide their email to be part of it.
- If it's a paid event, you get to generate additional income.
- You position yourself as a leader in your field.

Saying that, putting together your own collaborative event certainly takes effort. Yes, each person involved will (hopefully!) help with promotion, but you're the one who will be responsible for creating the vision, managing the logistics and making sure everything goes as planned.

The more people who are part of an event like this, the more moving pieces. In my experience, it's not easy, but the rewards can be great.

Let me give you some examples of collaborative events I've put together in my own business.

The Money Mastery Gathering

Back in 2015 when I pivoted into helping women business owners with their money mindset, I hosted this small online summit where I invited around six women in the field to be interviewed. Most I pre-recorded, but I did a couple live as well.

I followed the traditional summit model where when people signed up for free, they got access to each interview for 24 hours after it was released. If they wanted to keep them for longer, there was an upsell where they paid to have access to a bundle of the recordings.

The Magical Portal Project

This was a community project I put together in the year after we launched The Unbound Press. I asked 31 authors to contribute and share how writing their book had activated transformation in their life. Most wrote a short article and some I invited to be interviewed. One contribution was released each day during the project and people signed up to access them, along with a dedicated group where we could discuss the themes that were coming up.

Bring Your Book to Life Micro Audio Summit

For this, I was inspired by Wendy Breakstone and her Micro Audio Summit approach. The idea is to have a small group of contributors and to provide specific and implementable content.

I gathered a group of experts, some from within the Unbound Writing community and some from outside, to share guidance on different stages of the book-writing journey. Unlike the traditional summit model, all interviews are released on one day and anyone who signs up gets ongoing access, so there's no rush to listen in.

There were a number of results from each of these.

1) They grew my email list substantially.
2) I created deeper connections with many of the women who were part of each event.
3) I created deeper connections with many of the people in my audience who signed up for the events.
4) I got to be more deeply of service to my people.
5) Each one generated an additional flow of income, both directly and indirectly.

Note how I put the income piece last? There's a reason for that.

In my experience, if you host a collaborative event like this with the sole intention of making more money, you're missing the big picture (and the full range of abundance available to you). Yes, when I hosted The Magical Portal Project, I had my first ever 5-figure sales month, but the effects rippled out FAR beyond that. Hosting that event anchored my identity as someone who holds space for magical beings to write books – for everyone who signed up, for the contributors AND for myself. Up until then, if I'm being honest, I'd been feeling like an imposter. Who was I to run a publishing company and help aspiring authors?

Running The Magical Portal Project made me realise (remember) EXACTLY who I was to do this. Through my interactions and conversations with the 31 contributors, I recognised I had the experience and ability to hold powerful space for creativity and expression.

Imagine the impact hosting an event like this could have on you. Yes, there are challenges and it will stretch you. But it can also help you remember who you are (and what you're here to do). Taking the lead with a collaborative project like this can help you step more fully into an abundance of YOU.

Feeling inspired?

Take some time to feel into the possibilities. If you were to run a collaborative event, what would it look like:

What would the theme of your event be?

_____

_____

Online or in-person?

Would it consist of interviews, workshops/trainings or written contributions?

What's your intention for the event?

- For yourself

- For the contributors

- *For those who sign-up*

Who would you love to be involved?

How long would the event be?

Would it be paid or free to attend?

Would people have ongoing access to the contributions or limited time?

What would you invite people into as a next step?

Hopefully that's given you some juice to get started with creating your own collaboration. This really is a fantastic way to generate more momentum, connection AND abundance in your business.

So, what's the first step you could take? The invitation is to do it! And let the magic begin to unfold...

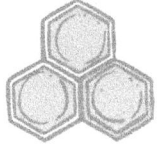

Creating a Platform for Your Readers & Clients

We already talked about creating a community experience for your people in the launching section. But having some kind of group or platform for your community isn't just for launching. Creating a space where you get to gather and connect more deeply is a powerful way to activate abundance for all involved.

When your people get to connect, not only with you, but with each other, true community begins to form. Ongoing relationships are created. Collaboration can be sparked through the different connections that are made. A group of like-hearted souls can be a beautiful thing.

So, how might you do this?

It could be something as simple as a Facebook group. I say Facebook, but as I'm writing this I know there are many different options here – Mighty Networks, Skool, Telegram, WhatsApp are just a few that come to mind. The question to ask is where do my people tend to naturally gather?

You could start some kind of in-person meet-up. In my experience, although being able to gather online is immensely powerful, people are craving in-person connection. If you were to offer this opportunity, even to a tiny group, who knows what magic it might spark?

I know many Unbound authors are attracted to the idea of creating a membership. This is something I've done a number of times over the years and as I write this I'm holding space for two – The Unbound Writer's Club and the Abundant Author Academy. This can be a powerful way to bring people together and share your magic in community.

Whether it's a free or paid space you create, I'd recommend keeping it simple to begin with.

What ideas do you have? What kind of community space are you feeling called to create?

The End?

We've been on quite the ride together haven't we, magical one?

Embodying the Abundant Author you are more fully, tuning into your intentions, embracing vibrant visibility, creating (and launching) a compelling offer and harnessing the power of community and collaboration. Whether you've already started taking action or are percolating on the possibilities, something has shifted.

My hope is that just reading this book has expanded your horizons and started to grow your capacity to experience more abundance in ALL ways.

And this is just the beginning.

The Abundant Author journey is never done.

Yes, you've reached the end of the book – go you! – but this process is designed for you to spiral around with it over and over (and over) again.

Earlier this morning, as I was out for a walk in the beautiful New Forest, not far from where I live, I was musing on the next evolution of my own Abundant Author journey. Like you, I'm a creative being. Ideas are always being sparked. And with each step, new clarity started to land about how I can refine an existing offer, making it more juicy and generous both for me and those step into it.

That's what I love about this path we're on. It's never a case of 'set it and forget it'. As we evolve and shift, so does our work and the way we share it.

For me, that feels deeply abundant.

We're shape-shifters.

Wayfinders.

Carving new ways as we go.

I'm excited to see what's next…

Here's to being the Abundant Author you're here to be.

Big love,

Nicola x

P.S. When I say 'I'm excited to see what's next', I mean it! I'd love to hear what this book has sparked off for you. Come find me on Instagram (I'm @nicolahumber) or pop me an email (nicola@nicolahumber.com).

P.P.S. Don't forget to check out your free Abundant Author bonus resources at: nicolahumber.com/abundant-author-resources

Acknowledgements

To Mr H, my partner on this unbound ride of life. I'm so grateful we get to grow together.

To my amazing sister, Louise, the first person I knew to start her own business and what a success it has been! Thank you for showing the way.

To my mum. Thanks for passing down your independent spirit and sense of adventure.

To Tonia G, my dear Sister Goddess. Our many conversations about abundance helped me to tap into what it truly means for me. I'm so glad we sat next to each other and connected all those years ago at Mastery in NYC.

To Sarah Lloyd, my roomie! I'm so grateful for our friendship and our mooches – they always spark off so much inspiration.

To Em, my partner in magic (and mayhem!) at The Unbound Press. I couldn't do it without you, beautiful soul.

To the whole Unbound team. Your support feels truly abundant and I'm SO grateful for each one of you.

To each one of my clients and members of the Unbound Writing community. You inspire me every single day. Thank you.

To the many teachers I've learned from over the years, too many to mention although some have been named in this book. We never create in isolation and the inspiration and support I've received along the way has been such a big part of the Abundant Author journey for me.

About the Author

Nicola Humber is the author of three other transformational books, *Heal Your Inner Good Girl*, *UNBOUND* and *Unbound Writing*, and creator of the #unbound365 journal.

She's also the founder of The Unbound Press, a soul-led publishing imprint for unbound women.

After playing the archetypal good girl up until her mid-thirties, Nicola left her 'proper' job in finance to retrain as a coach and hypnotherapist and this leap of faith led her to what she does now: activating recovering good girls to embrace their so-called imperfections and shake off the tyranny of 'shoulds', so they can be their fullest, freest, most magnificent selves.

Nicola helps women to write the book their Unbound Self is calling them to write, whilst growing a community of soul-family readers and clients.

She's also the host of The Unbound Writer's Club podcast.

Find out more at: nicolahumber.com

www.ingramcontent.com/pod-product-compliance
Lightning Source LLC
Chambersburg PA
CBHW041307110526
44590CB00028B/4274